IN THE KENNEDY STYLE

IN THE KENNEDY STYLE

MAGICAL EVENINGS
IN THE KENNEDY WHITE HOUSE

BY LETITIA BALDRIGE
MENUS AND RECIPES BY WHITE HOUSE
CHEF RENÉ VERDON

A MADISON PRESS BOOK

DESIGNED AND PRODUCED FOR

DOUBLEDAY
NEW YORK, LONDON, TORONTO

Doubleday
A Division of Bantam Doubleday Dell Publishing Group, Inc.
1540 Broadway
New York, N.Y. 10036
U.S.A.

Library of Congress Cataloging-in-Publication Data

Baldrige, Letitia
In the Kennedy style : magical evenings in the Kennedy White House /
by Letitia Baldrige ; menus and recipes by White House Chef René Verdon.
p.   cm.
ISBN 0-385-48964-1 (hardcover)
1. Dinners and dining. 2. Menus.
3. Kennedy, John F. (John Fitzgerald), 1917-1963.
4. Onassis, Jacqueline Kennedy, 1929-1994. I. Verdon, Rene, 1924- . II. Title.
TX 737.B38 1998
642'.4—dc21   97-39466   CIP

Produced by
Madison Press Books
40 Madison Avenue
Toronto, Ontario
Canada M5R 2S1

Printed and bound in Great Britain

*For all those
who have heard
about the grace and
charm of the
Kennedy White House
and wondered,
was it really that
extraordinary?
The answer is "Yes."*

— Letitia Baldrige

*To the memory
of President
John F. Kennedy and
Mrs. Kennedy.
The days I spent
as their White House
chef were golden
and filled with joy
and pride.*

— René Verdon

CONTENTS

FOREWORD

❧

ORKING IN THE KENNEDY WHITE HOUSE was the best time of my life. It would be a magical experience for any chef to know that the meals he created would be served in the most famous house in the world to some of the most famous people in the world, from Pablo Casals to Princess Grace of Monaco. But what made those White House years truly memorable for me was the graciousness and warmth of the wonderful couple who headed that household — and indeed the country. I have many fabulous memories of them and the time we spent together. Some are of intimate family moments — the President, dressed in slippers and Bermuda shorts, trimming his son's hair in the upstairs kitchen while Mrs. Kennedy laughingly critiqued the procedure. Others are of gala state occasions — the menus we planned for them and the pride we would all feel when our plans succeeded.

Mind you, my first day at the White House didn't begin very auspiciously. A snowstorm delayed my bus from New York, and I arrived three hours late for my meeting with Mrs. Kennedy. One of the first people I met after I arrived at the White House was Letitia Baldrige, the social secretary. I was half expecting a chilly welcome because I was late, but Miss Baldrige was very kind and it was not long before I was calling her Tish like everyone else. Mrs. Kennedy also made me feel right at home. Both spoke French to me because my English at that time was not very good. "With the weather so bad, how did you get here?" asked Mrs. Kennedy. And I remember saying, "I think every man can make an effort for the First Lady of the United States."

Later I was shown the room that would be my home for the next five years. It was a comfortable room on the third floor, just above the floor where the Kennedys lived. The following day Mrs. Kennedy brought the President to the kitchen to meet me, a moment I will never forget. He, too, spoke French — or at least tried to — while his lovely wife looked on and smiled at his efforts. Those first meetings set the tone for our working relationship, one based on mutual respect.

To prepare for state dinners, I would sometimes spend fourteen to sixteen hours in the kitchen. Mrs. Kennedy always sent a personal thank-you note afterward, mostly proclaiming the meal a great success. President Kennedy sometimes came into the kitchen afterward and thanked the staff, too. The Kennedys had very specific likes and dislikes, but even when they were displeased, they were pleasant and courteous. I particularly remember one time the President asked to see me.

"Chef," he said, "I like my steak broiled, medium rare."

"But it is broiled, Mr. President," I answered.

"Well, it looks fried to me," he insisted. "It's shiny on top."

"That's because I brushed the top with a little butter," I explained. "Look, sir, you can see the marks of the grill on the steak."

He smiled and said, "I guess you're right. Thank you, Chef."

As the months went by, he was less formal and began to call me René, as Mrs. Kennedy did.

At that time America wasn't known for its cooking. People talked about gravies, not sauces. The Kennedys, though, were a cosmopolitan couple who loved and knew good food. Through their state dinners and private dinner parties, they helped introduce French cuisine to the American people. In fact, Julia Child once said that if I hadn't been in the White House, she would not have sold so many cookbooks!

Working on this book has brought back a flood of memories. After I sent my first cookbook to Mrs. Kennedy, she sent me a letter saying, "I remember when Caroline and I invaded your kitchen to bake little pink cupcakes hard as rocks from a toy baking set that she had gotten for her fifth birthday — and you were as concerned as if it had been a soufflé for a State Dinner." We won't be able to share memories this time, but I do think she would have joined me in my hope that *In the Kennedy Style* will inspire its readers and help them recreate some of the magic of the Kennedy years in their own homes.

— René Verdon,
White House Chef

America in 1961 was entranced by the style of its new president and his beautiful young wife.

THAT SPECIAL STYLE

"What endures from

the Kennedy era are those dazzling evenings of culture,

fostered and inspired by Jackie...."

— Jamie Auchincloss

IT WAS A PERFECT JULY DAY, AND BELOW ME THE California seacoast glittered in sunshine. Reluctantly I turned my gaze to the typewriter. I had determined that I would devote my vacation to working on a novel and had selected a friend's house on Partington Ridge above Big Sur as the perfect place to do this. Perhaps the nearby presence of Henry Miller and other renowned artists and neighbors would serve to inspire me. Instead I felt like an ant toiling in a field of giants. The sound of the telephone brought welcome distraction.

The caller's voice was pitched high, like an exuberant schoolgirl's, and there was such a babble of voices in the background I could barely make out her words.

"Can you believe that Jack made it?" the voice asked. "He really made it! Will you come to the White House to help us out? Will you head up my staff? We're really going to need you."

It was Jacqueline Bouvier Kennedy calling from Hyannisport. Only the week before, her husband had won the Democratic Presidential nomination. I was thrilled for her, delighted for the senator, and enormously proud for the entire Kennedy-Bouvier-Auchincloss clan. But the job offer didn't seem real because I didn't believe that Jack could ever win. There are stars and superstars, and John F. Kennedy obviously was one of the latter, but a young Catholic to be elected President of the United States? In July of 1960, this seemed an impossibly long shot.

Even at eighteen, Jackie's natural sense of style (left) was apparent. (Top) In August 1949, Jackie (at center) departed for her year at the Sorbonne. While working as the Inquiring Photographer for the Washington Times-Herald in 1951 (above), she met Jack Kennedy and by the summer of 1953 (opposite) they were engaged.

I had known Jackie since our teens. I was three years ahead of her at Miss Porter's School in Farmington, Connecticut, and at Vassar College. My parents were friends of her mother and stepfather, Janet and Hugh Auchincloss, and I went to parties at Merrywood, their home in McLean, Virginia, where the glamorous Bouvier sisters turned every head. I remember Hugh Auchincloss sighing at one of the parties, "If this place were three times the size it is, I still couldn't get enough sleep, considering the noise made throughout the entire house until breakfast time."

Jackie was named Debutante of the Year in 1947, and young men were constantly trying every kind of trick to make her go out with them. Her classic good looks were complemented by her sense of style, which had been apparent from her early teens. She would buy a simple dress or skirt or pants and shirt, add the perfect belt and then make the whole outfit look even better

because of her posture and the way she moved in it. Nothing ever looked wrong on her.

After Vassar, I went to work for Ambassador and Mrs. David Bruce in Paris, and soon Jackie arrived there to study at the Sorbonne. Later, when I was home on leave from my embassy post and Jackie was doing her photo-reporter work in Washington, we had lunch and reminisced about Paris. It was then that I first saw the excitement in her eyes when she talked about a young senator she had started dating named Jack Kennedy. I could tell she was smitten. But so were many other young women. Jack Kennedy was considered a "really tasty number." (Translation: "He had everything.") I had known him since the beginning of my Paris diplomatic experience. Rose Kennedy and her daughters would also visit Paris periodically, and the American embassy would always show the flag for them because of Papa Joe Kennedy's political clout. I arranged dates for the girls with attractive young

Policemen held back the crowds as the newly married couple descended the steps of St. Mary's Church, Newport, Rhode Island, on the morning of September 12, 1953. The reception took place at the Auchincloss estate on Narragansett Bay and after an outdoor luncheon, the bridal party (below) posed for photographs.

French friends of mine, who took them out to dinner in the best restaurants and dancing in the romantic *boîtes de nuit* like Monseigneur. (After strong complaints from my friends that they were always stuck with the bills, which were astronomical, I became savvy enough to demand cash in advance from Joe Kennedy's office to pay for the expensive dates *avec les filles* Kennedy.)

A little more than a year after our lunch, while I was in Rome working for Ambassador Clare Boothe Luce, Jackie married her handsome senator. Now she had her first real home of her own, a house in Georgetown that she did over to her own taste — showing a preference for pastel colors, beautiful fabrics, floral prints, and delicate porcelains. Although she never had to cook, she knew that important men would come to her house in Georgetown to enjoy themselves and make meaningful conversation if she offered them good food. Aware of her husband's ambitions, she was ready to help. If she was upset by the earthy politicians who inhabited her living room day and night, smoking cigars, littering the floor with papers and leaking pens, resting their dirty shoes on her beautiful antique coffee table, she never showed what she was thinking. A smile would appear around her mouth while her eyes flashed warning thunder signs. Only those close to her knew what that smile meant. When the visitors ground out their cigarettes in her crystal glasses and mashed their olive pits and cracker crumbs into her beautiful handmade Spanish and Portuguese rugs, she bit her lip. The smile would reappear. She was a politician's wife. They were headed for impossible pastures. It was worth anything to her husband, and it became worth anything to her, too.

After the wedding, the young couple lived with their respective in-laws until Jackie insisted they find a place of their own. Their first home was a small, rented house on Dent Place in Georgetown. In April of 1954, photographer Orlando Suero persuaded Jack Kennedy to be the subject of a photo essay on the daily life of a young, rising senator. For several days he followed the Kennedys around, documenting their home life, JFK working in his Senate office, and Jackie attending classes at Georgetown University. Here, Suero recorded Jackie preparing for the first formal dinner party in her new home with housekeeper Mattie Penn, and then in one magical shot, captured her lighting the dinner candles.

"I remember that when she got the N Street house,
it was going to be just right. It was a house with a lot
of feeling about it and a lot of charm...."

— Janet Lee Auchincloss

❧

The creation of a new home in Georgetown and the birth
of Caroline in November of 1957 ushered in a happy period for the
Kennedy marriage. Jackie was persuaded to pose for these 1959
photographs to help build her husband's national profile before a
planned presidential run the following year.

WITHIN A WEEK OF JACKIE'S CALL TO ME my skepticism changed to wholehearted belief in Jack's ability to grab the brass ring. Everyone in the media seemed suddenly to belong to JFK's own public relations firm. His face and name were everywhere. He was young, handsome, sexy, and intelligent, too. In the ensuing three months, I bid adieu to Big Sur and my great novel, resigned from my job as director of public relations for Tiffany's in New York, officially changed my voter registration from Republican to Democrat, and volunteered to help get Jack elected. Once I'd decided that JFK would win, I never doubted it for a moment; such is the psychology of partisanship.

Two weeks after the election I was officially appointed social secretary to the First Lady-elect, but I'd been on the job since the moment the final (razor-close) tally had been announced. Even though Jackie was almost eight months pregnant and had just endured an election campaign, she was on the phone to me constantly from her Georgetown house. (Until I found a Washington apartment in January, I camped with my parents.) No detail of her impending job escaped her notice, right down to the design of her official stationery. I burned up the typewriter with notes on decisions she made or had to make. On top of my real job, it sometimes seemed that members of the Kennedy clan were on the phone to me every hour on the hour with a question or a request. It's a good thing I've never needed much sleep, because it was a "Got a problem? Call Tish" period of two and a half months.

In one of Jackie's telephone calls, she asked me to describe briefly the interior of the President's Mansion, as the living and reception areas in the central part of the house were called (as distinct from the East and West wings, where the offices are housed). All I remember of my answer to Jackie's question was that I described it as a conglomeration. In fact, it is a very strange place to serve as a home. The President and his family live on an upper story of a building that is flanked by wings of offices. Each day hundreds of people, if not thousands, tramp through the corridor that connects the East Wing offices and the West Wing offices. Thus the appellation goldfish bowl is an apt one to describe the living circumstances of any presidential family. A house is certainly not a home in this instance — more like a "porticoed temple buttressed by two train stations," as a staff member once described it.

Fewer than three weeks after the election, on November 25, 1960, Jackie gave birth to her second child — a one-month premature baby boy — at Georgetown Hospital. The dramatic appearance of John F. Kennedy, Jr., made the weeks leading up to the inauguration even more of a challenge. Having been clobbered by the aftereffects of the baby's cesarean birth, Jackie was too exhausted to concentrate on intricate scheduling plans. Press hysteria rose to greater heights, and we were swamped by people who were close and not close to Jackie, all demanding to see her and the baby.

It was important for the new mother to get some rest, and the answer to all requests to talk to her or see her was an identical no, but there were varying layers of diplomatic coatings on each refusal. You can't say no to the dean of the diplomatic corps with the same dispatch that you say it to a bridge partner of baby John's grandmother. It helped that a few days after they left the hospital, Jackie and the baby were on their way to Palm Beach, Florida, where Jackie could recuperate.

During the 1960 race for the Democratic nomination, Jackie proved an effective campaigner, particularly in the pivotal state of West Virginia (above), where JFK overtook his chief rival, Hubert Humphrey. But in the fall presidential campaign (below, left and right), her pregnancy limited her campaign appearances.

*Caroline looks up from her baby brother at photographer Richard Avedon during a photo
session in January of 1961. Although Jackie was very protective of her children's privacy, she realized
that pictures helped to satisfy the enormous public interest in them.*

Before departing for Florida, Jackie accepted Mamie Eisenhower's belated invitation to visit the White House for an introductory tour. As is so often the case, the meeting between the outgoing First Lady, in this case old enough to be Jackie's mother, and the First Lady-elect was awkward. Jackie's post-operative condition made it agony for her. The wheelchair she had requested remained hidden behind a door, waiting for her to ask for it. (She later confessed she'd been too shy to do so and that the ordeal had sent her back to bed for two weeks once she got to Palm Beach.) But she seems to have left an impression on Mrs. Eisenhower, who commented to J.B. West, the chief usher, "There certainly are going to be some changes made around here!"

Not long after John's birth, Jackie returned to writing short notes and voluminous memos on her notepads, keeping lists, making recommendations, posing questions, and often answering them herself before she got to the end. She knew her strong suits and she would capitalize on them as First Lady to help her husband. "The entertaining is going to be very important to us," she said in one telephone call. "There are many things that can be done to make it warmer, more gracious, more distinguished." She had become a superb hostess in her married life. To entertain on a much grander scale but with the same personal flair was a challenge she clearly relished.

During early January, while Jackie recuperated

in Palm Beach and bombarded me with memos, I was sheepishly engaged in a covert operation with Chief Usher J. B. West, in effect the CEO of the White House staff. He had agreed to smuggle into the mansion bags and boxes of personal effects the Kennedys would need on inauguration day, which were discreetly tucked away in his secret storerooms.

The White House officially changes hands at

A few days after his birth, John Jr., was christened in the chapel of Georgetown Hospital in the same embroidered gown his father had once worn.

twelve noon on inauguration day. At 12:01, while the rest of the country was at the Capitol, either in person or glued to their TV sets for the swearing in, a small procession of White House cars passed through the south gates of the White House grounds, bearing Mrs. Kennedy's maid, Provie (Providencia Parades), the President's valet, George

"Let the word go forth from this time and place...

that the torch has been passed to a new generation...."

— President John F. Kennedy in his inauguration speech

Thomas, me and my files, and the presidential couple's finery for that evening's balls. (We also carried the more pedestrian necessities, such as pajamas, a nightgown and bathrobes, a makeup case for the First Lady, and the items to be placed in their respective medicine cabinets.) Caroline, baby John, the nurse, and their Secret Serviceman were in Palm Beach at the Kennedy grandparents' house and would come to their new home a few days later.

I remember during the car ride how carefully Provie had covered Mrs. Kennedy's white ballgown and the cape she would wear that night. No wedding dress was attracting more international attention that year. (As it turned out, Jackie much preferred the elegantly simple white satin gown by Oleg Cassini that she wore to the gala the night before the inaugura-

While JFK delivered his historic address (above), I was in the White House preparing for the arrival of the Kennedys. (Opposite) That evening, Jackie left to attend the inaugural balls, wearing the gown we had carefully carried into the White House at noon.

inaugural ballgowns instead of the Bergdorf gown.)

As we drove up the long, curving driveway, the sun reflected jagged rays of blinding light on the fresh snow everywhere. The house, with its new coats of white paint, was so dazzling, we could not make out its architectural details. It was a surreal scene against a tanzanite blue sky.

J.B. West stood with his hand outstretched at the southwest door, his face warm and welcoming. He greeted us as he and previous chief ushers had been greeting new presidential staffs through history. Provie asked in wonder, "How did he know the exact moment we would arrive and be there to greet us?" What Provie didn't know is that every time anyone comes

tion to the Bergdorf-designed gown in which she appeared at the inaugural balls. She called the Cassini ballgown "my favorite dress of all time" and wanted it to appear in the Smithsonian's display of

into the private part of the White House or leaves it, the usher's office is notified of the precise movements of people and cars. Even emergency bathroom visits are factored in to the advance schedule. Many such secrets of life in America's most famous

house were about to be revealed to me.

I had entered the White House before, always as a guest, but had never lost my awe of it. My first visit was in 1931, during the Hoover administration, when I was four years old, and I remember the episode vividly. Our parents took me and my older brothers, Mac and Bob, to the White House Easter party for congressmen and their children. (My father was a Republican congressman from Nebraska.) I huffed and puffed with indignation at my brothers' terrible manners that day. They ran a race to see who could consume the greatest number of orange juices and cookies being passed in the East Room on silver trays by white-gloved footmen. At the age of four, I was already embarked on a career of teaching manners. I tattled on my brothers' gross behavior to our parents, for which indiscretion my brothers wrought revenge on me for months to come.

My most recent visit had been in 1958, when Mrs. Eisenhower had graciously permitted Tiffany's to borrow some historic pieces of vermeil (silver-gilt hollowware from the eighteenth and nineteenth centuries) for an important historic exhibit. I'm sure the loan was eased by my personal connection to the Eisenhowers through a friend of my parents', General Al Gruenther, who was Ike's great pal. It was on that 1958 visit that I first met J.B. West and became acquainted with the character of the house with all its nooks and crannies. The two days spent cataloguing the White House vermeil collection laid the foundation of my friendship with J.B., who would become a firm ally in getting things done in the Kennedy White House.

THE CHILDREN COME FIRST

It had been many years since a president with young children had lived in the White House and the novelty of this captivated the American public. "I have suddenly realized what it means to completely lose one's privacy," wrote Jackie in a first letter to her press secretary, Pam Turnure. Jackie was determined that her schedule not jeopardize her time with the children and it was often a challenge for me to get her to focus on official White House business.

British nanny Maud Shaw firmly believed in fresh air for baby John (above). (Opposite) The American public couldn't get enough of photographs like this one.

JACQUELINE KENNEDY WAS WELL GROUNDED in the essential ingredients of giving a good party. But her first dinner party in the White House, on Sunday night, January 22, proved that she had her work as a hostess cut out for her. The Kennedys dined with five close friends, including Mr. and Mrs. Franklin D. Roosevelt, Jr., in what was called the Family Dining Room, with its gloomy burgundy curtains and carpet. What should have been an evening of easy conviviality was marred by poor food served in a cold and damp room — there wasn't a fireplace lit in the house — with the voices of the diners echoing loudly from the high ceiling.

After dinner, while the women retired to the equally cold Green Room for coffee, the men went in search of a restroom. They wandered from room to room, with everyone berating FDR, Jr., for not knowing where a bathroom was located. After all, he had spent many years in this house. They finally concluded there was no such room on the main reception floor, so FDR, Jr., was forgiven. (There is no powder room on the main floor to this day.)

That first dinner made the Kennedys realize that giving even a small party in the White House is, of course, a giant challenge in comparison to having twelve people for dinner in a Georgetown home. It is rather easy to be a First Lady who turns over every detail to her well-trained staff and does not give an upcoming event a further thought. It is much more difficult to be a First Lady who puts her stamp on every aspect of entertaining. Jacqueline Kennedy was one of the latter.

As the months went on, I watched her become more and more skilled in dealing with the small, personal details that warm up a cold, official function. Attending a White House dinner can be exactly like attending a formal banquet in a large commercial hotel. But in the Kennedy years, the guests were every minute aware that they were in someone's home, albeit a rather grand one. It was something Jackie wanted to do: establish an atmosphere of warmth, a mood that put guests at their ease — a play of dim lights, music and the mixed fragrances of the flowers everywhere, the women's perfume, and the smell of herbs and sauces from the kitchen.

One of the earliest signs that entertaining would be different in the Kennedy White House came only one week later, on January 29, when the house opened for the first public party. It was an excited and enthusiastic group of guests who wandered through the entire main floor. The invitees included Cabinet officers, leaders of Congress, the other presidential appointees, and the politicos and fund-raisers who'd helped get the president elected, along with their families. We also invited certain members of the press corps.

Naturally, I assumed that alcohol was to be served at such a gathering, so I ordered good-quality brands of liquor to complement the hors d'oeuvres. But the usher's office promptly informed me that under the previous administration they didn't serve hard liquor at large parties; they served a spiked punch and a nonalcoholic fruit punch. I replied that the Kennedys wanted to entertain well and that they wouldn't hear of such a thing. So I surged ahead and had a bar set up in the Family Dining Room and another in the East Room.

The party was a smash. The Marine Band played selections from Jerome Kern and Cole Porter, and the liquor flowed freely. But next morning I

As White House social secretary, my duties could range from arranging a tea with Jackie for American museum directors (above) to handing out candy canes at a children's Christmas party (right).

∞

"Well, Mr. President," I replied, "you said you wanted a good party, and I just arranged it that way."

This did not placate him. He dressed me down — it wouldn't be for the last time, either — and I promised to consult him before I made any other such momentous decisions. (I told my staff, "I've already had my timbers shivered.") But exactly one year later, he stopped me in the corridor and said, "You know, I've been meaning to say something to you, Tish." (The President used to consult his old journal each day to check what had happened the year previously.)

"What would that be, Mr. President?" I asked, more than curious.

"Today's the anniversary of our first reception. The fact that you put one over on us and served hard liquor at that first party — and we have been serving it ever since — was the greatest thing that's ever been done for White House entertaining. It's relaxed the whole thing, and you've proved it to be a great success, and I just want to say thank you."

discovered I had created the first *scandale* of the new regime. "Liquor in the White House," the headlines screamed. *Le tout* Washington talked of nothing else, and the President got an earful from Bible Belt congressmen and temperance organizations.

The next day he called me in an absolute rage. "What did you do to me?" he thundered. "Why did you do it? Isn't this job difficult enough without you alienating an entire section of America?"

That's one reason we all loved him so much. He could dress us down, but he always remembered to pay us compliments when we deserved them.

By spring we were running at full speed, planning for a series of high-level visits and several foreign trips. Upcoming-events files covered every inch of furniture and all the windowsills in my office. But the most pressing item on my desk was the impending state dinner for President Habib Bourguiba of Tunisia, who would be the first leader so honored during the Kennedy years.

For this dinner unlike all subsequent such evenings, the President, rather than Jackie, called the shots. President Kennedy, who loved all things military, felt that Bourguiba would be most interested in and impressed with a well-orchestrated spectacle of military pomp. This idea worried State Department Chief of Protocol Angier Biddle Duke, so he checked with the Tunisian ambassador to the United States, who came back with the response, "Wonderful idea!" The President's military aides took over the program, and I remember Jackie saying to me at one point, "Never have I felt so out of control of a party. This is like a military engagement, and you and I are just civilians, behind the front lines."

The night of May 3, 1961, was memorable for many reasons. It was the first and last state dinner in the Kennedy administration to be served at the traditional U-shaped table. The weather in early May is usually bordering on hot, but that year, as luck would have it, May 3 was an unusually damp, cold night. Women had not worn their furs, because everyone had stored them for the season. Most came without wraps and wearing décolleté ball gowns. After dinner, shivering guests were given blankets as they took their seats on the lawn for the military show by the south entrance. We realized then, and many other times to come, that one does not control Mother Nature. She pays no respect to heads of state.

At our first state dinner, held in honor of President and Mrs. Bourguiba of Tunisia, Jackie wore a yellow one-shouldered "Nefertiti" gown designed by Oleg Cassini. (Opposite) After dinner the two presidents and their wives watched the military review from the first-floor balcony while their guests shivered below.

The President's aides had served him well. President Bourguiba stood ramrod straight on the first-floor balcony, mesmerized by the great show of flash and color. Four hundred eighty men participated (no marching women in those days), including the crack Marine drill squad, twirling and precision slapping their rifles; two units of marchers; and the bands from all the services, most notably the Air Force band, resplendent in kilts. They put on a glorious show while great searchlights wove patterns in the sky.

The next day the President called in his aides, congratulated them on the stunning spectacle they had arranged, and then produced an unexpected explosion of the famous Kennedy temper. "When President Bourguiba and I passed down the line of marchers, inspecting the troops, never have I seen so many men who were flabby and out of shape, with bad skin and thick glasses. The Marines, on the other hand, were in perfect shape. They looked like supermen. All I can say is, in future military reviews, I want the Marines up front. You can hide the others." At least on this occasion, I wasn't the target of the President's wrath. (The Army, Navy, and Air Force eventually managed to get their troops back into the front lines for dress parades — the perfect male specimens, that is!)

I may have broken the sound barrier when it came to serving alcohol at the White House, but it was Jackie who transformed the archaic set-in-stone traditions of White House entertaining into new, dynamic, and flexible directions. As First Lady, she was determined to make the executive mansion

Round tables in the repainted State Dining Room (opposite) created a more intimate mood at dinners such as this one held for JFK's sister Jean and her husband, Stephen Smith. (Above) Jackie liked the conviviality created by rather close table settings (above) and also favored simpler and more natural flower arrangements (below).

almost as welcoming as she had her Georgetown house. No easy task when you have hundreds of guests milling about. But what a revolution in entertaining the Kennedys wrought.

As long as anyone could remember, state dinners, which were held in the gloomy State Dining Room with its vast bronze chandelier and lugubrious green walls, had been stiff and stuffy affairs, with the guests seated around a single horseshoe-shaped table or, occasionally, at a long rectangular table covered in formal white linen. In certain administrations an enormous E-shaped table filled the room, with towering urns of flowers down the center, guaranteeing that most guests wouldn't be able to see either the room or each other.

Jackie ordered that the room be repainted and the seating arrangements changed. The dark green walls and moldings were to be painted two tones of white — all the better to bring out the beauty and detail of the intricate carvings — which made the room seem brighter, lighter, and more welcoming. And henceforth White House guests would sit at round tables for eight or ten — never twelve, as hotels often use, which make conversation more awkward. Circular buttercup-yellow or pale-blue linen cloths were made, sometimes with overcloths of white organdy. Not only did this arrangement nearly double the number of guests that could be accommodated, it created the intimacy and conviviality of smaller groupings. In the rare event there had to be a head table, a single long table that seated twenty-two was used.

Into this setting Jackie introduced flower arrangements reminiscent of great Flemish still lifes, natural, subtle, and relaxed. "The opposite," as the First Lady commented, "of what you'd find in a funeral home when a prominent person dies." The flowers in the table centerpiece baskets were cut low, so that no one's vision of the great dining room would be in any way obscured. The colors of the flowers in vases and cachepots scattered throughout the reception rooms and hallways were chosen to enhance the paintings that hung above them, or to match the color of the wall fabrics in that particular room. The flowers were also selected to lend a great fragrance to the large spaces — and to help combat the smell of tobacco, which, in those smoking permitted days, clung to the damask draperies, the rugs, and the upholstery fabrics.

Great care was taken to make certain the tables were set to perfection. The white tapers were burned for ten minutes before they were lit for the actual dinner so that they could be checked for tilting and so that the wicks would be black, not waxy white. Every piece of flatware was polished before it was set on the tablecloth and positioned exactly where it was meant to be. Every piece of crystal was carefully inspected for spots. Each guest found a heavy white stock menu at his or her place, listing the courses and the wines in calligraphy and bearing the presidential seal embossed in gold at the top. The matching place card with its presidential seal bore the guest's name, also written in calligraphy. Savvy guests,

René Verdon confers with Anne Lincoln (above), who was in charge of the household staff. René's menus (left) were at first written in French but after criticism that the White House was becoming "too French," menus became anglicized and American wines more prominent.

mindful of history, would send their menu cards around their table and have each guest sign the back — a perfect souvenir. There was a vermeil ashtray at each place, with an accompanying white or black book of matches, its cover adorned with the gold presidential seal. (In the Kennedy years, guests loved to take those matchbooks away with them as souvenirs; some of them took the costly ashtrays, too, but in today's smokeless world, they are no longer around to be snitched.)

But none of these details would have meaning if the food didn't match their importance. Thanks to chef René Verdon, it did. Perhaps more than any other President and First Lady in history, John and Jacqueline Kennedy cared about food. They wanted to offer their guests great cuisine and *tous les plaisirs de la table*. And this meant hiring a great chef.

René Verdon was a classically trained exponent of French haute cuisine and came well recommended by the owners of La Caravelle, one of the favorite Kennedy restaurants in New York. He and his pastry chef, Ferdinand Louvat, soon had the kitchen humming. They chose top people to assist them and before long were known by reputation to every chef in America. They earned far less than the commercial chefs in town, or even the embassy chefs, but they were at the undisputed summit of their professions.

UNDER THE KENNEDYS, A STATE DINNER BECAME a carefully choreographed evening of fine food and entertainment. As guests stepped into the entrance on the ground floor, they heard the sounds of the Marine Orchestra playing in the central hall upstairs. After checking their coats, they mounted a marble staircase to the main floor as the music filled every room of the mansion.

While the guests mingled in the East Room and enjoyed a pre-dinner cocktail, the Kennedys entertained the state visitor and his wife in the Yellow Oval Room, a former study on the second floor that Jackie had converted into the living room of their private quarters. Just outside it Jackie would have cunningly placed all the official gifts, so that she and the President could comment on them as they entered. Then they would have a quiet cocktail with their honored guests and their two countries' ambassadors, along with the Secretary of State and Mrs. Rusk, and perhaps the chief of protocol and his wife.

At about eight-thirty, when the chief usher had checked with the chef and the head butler to make certain that all was in readiness, I would give the order to the head of the color guard. He would come upstairs into the Yellow Oval Room, salute, and say, "Mr. President, may I take the colors?" The president would nod, and the color guard would form outside the door. Then, accompanied by the color guard, the Kennedys and their official guests would descend the stairs in a grand march to the first floor. At the bottom of the stairs they would pause to have their pictures taken by press photographers. At the first strains of "Hail to the Chief," the President was supposed to lead the way into the East Room, where the other guests were gathered.

The only difficulty with this scenario was that the President was a fast mover. In his impatience, he was always moving off before the media had finished their picture taking. It was embarrassing for me to chase after him when he did not follow the script — I had to grab his arm and guide him back

to the stairs. Sometimes he headed in the wrong direction, into an unused room. Quite early in his tenure he said, "I've got a new name for you: it's Miss Push-and-Pull."

On one occasion — I think it was the visit of an African president — he came down the elevator to the first floor to show his guest around before the official part of the evening began, and I heard him say, "Now, Mr. President, I want to show you our very handsome house." With that he walked into the butler's pantry, where the staff, coatless, with sleeves rolled up, and smoking cigarettes, were preparing the cocktails! As he backed out unceremoniously, he said to me, "So, this isn't

where we are supposed to be. Maybe after a few more months in this place I'll learn the floor plan." Eventually he learned to look over and catch my eye, and I would signal with my hands to indicate which direction he should take. But he never got over the habit of rushing ahead of his wife, leaving her looking alone and forgotten. (She was used to it and was often amused by his impetuousness. It was just JFK being JFK.)

In the East Room, the guests were introduced to the Kennedys and the visiting head of state and his spouse in a fast-moving receiving line. If anyone insisted on holding up the line, we would approach from behind and force them to move on in a kind

A state dinner, like the one shown opposite for King Hassan of Morocco, usually began with the official party posing at the bottom of the stairs. (Left) In characteristic style, JFK heads off on his own after posing with Harry Truman. Then came the receiving line before dinner (top right). After the evening's performance, it was a thrill (right) to introduce the performers.

of strong, diplomatic body language. As the guests came off the line, they were ushered directly to the State Dining Room through the Green, Blue and Red Rooms.

The Kennedys disliked having to talk to their guests of honor over music, even soft music. The acoustics in the State Dining Room were such that when it was full, quiet conversation could be difficult. As the dessert course neared its end, in from the kitchen would burst a single file of Air Force Strolling Strings, playing their signature, energetic Gypsy music with such passion and vigor that many of the guests wanted to leap up and do some spontaneous dancing on the spot. After this, the tempo

changed to soft, romantic tunes, and by the time the meal had ended, they had played themselves out of the dining room and into the big, red-carpeted hallway. The Kennedys and their visiting heads of state rose and walked out of the dining room, the signal for their guests to follow. The Strings lined up on both sides of the corridor, playing away with gusto, while the waiters passed through the crowd with trays of demitasses, glasses of champagne, or water (not "designer water", but good old 1960s tap water). The hosts and guests chatted and walked through the reception rooms of the main floor until it was time to go into the East Room, set up with little gold chairs for the evening's entertainment.

"Mrs. Kennedy had such marvelous taste...

that all the women across the country, copied her... that little pillbox...

the sleeveless shift. It was epidemic, that wardrobe."

— Betty Ford

The President was extremely proud of the performances by distinguished artists, but he always asked the same questions before each event: "How

fast can you get the program started?" and "How long is tonight's entertainment going to last?" "That's too long," he would say before I had a chance to answer. "You always promise it won't last longer than twenty-five minutes, and then it goes on and on. Please, do what I ask and make them cut the length of their performance!" The President, with a hurting back, was eager to have the evening come to its conclusion. He always had briefing papers to go over in preparation for the next day. But it was very difficult for me to tell artists such as

Pablo Casals and Isaac Stern to please step on it.

In any case, the Kennedys made history with their after-dinner performances in the East Room and proudly showed off the best of the best to the world. Theirs was the first administration to showcase writers and poets and to present great performing artists from the theater, ballet, opera, and concert halls on a stage we had specially built for the East Room.

It only took about three weeks after the inauguration for those of us in the White House to realize that in Jacqueline Kennedy we had a huge star on our hands. Women were writing to the White House asking for the name of her brand of shampoo and exactly how many rollers she used when she went to bed, and did the President object? They wanted to know the color of her lipstick and what baby food she fed John, Jr.

The letters and gifts poured into the East Wing by the vanload, nine thousand a week. I showed her a sampling of the really amusing ones (such as a portrait done of her with sticky caramel corn, her mouth drawn with red nail polish) and the kind,

It was on the first state visit to Canada that we became aware of the public's enormous interest in Jackie, seen above with Madame Vanier, wife of Canada's governor general, and, below, in a show-stopping red wool suit inspired by the uniforms of the Royal Canadian Mounted Police.

sweet notes ("If I could be one-half as good a mother to my children as you are to yours . . ."). Pam Turnure, the bright young press secretary, sent her the complimentary press clippings and spared her the few mean-spirited ones. Pam had a tough job because the press wanted access to Mrs. Kennedy day and night, and Pam's assignment was to fend them off, to keep the children out of the press, and yet keep good stories coming.

But we didn't realize the degree of Jackie's rising stardom until the state visit to Canada in May 1961. It was the Kennedys' first official foreign trip and the first time we saw how people outside the United States felt about our first couple. A month or so before our departure, the Canadian ambassador to Washington paid me a solemn visit to prepare us all for an unemotional reaction in the Canadian capital. Canadians aren't as demonstrative as Americans, he explained. "In fact," he added sadly, "the Queen is always prepared for — but a trifle upset by — the cool reception she receives in Ottawa."

Along the route the presidential motorcade took from the Ottawa airport to Rideau Hall, the Governor-General's residence where the Kennedys and a small number of us were to stay, masses of people applauded and cheered. And through the chorus came the rhythmic chant of "Jack-ie! Jack-ie!" Our hosts, Governor General and Madame Vanier, were dumbfounded — they'd never seen anything like it before — and we were elated.

But nothing could equal the visit to France a few weeks later, which was subsequently referred to as the Jackie French Trip. The emotions I felt watching the motorcade carry the de Gaulles and the Kennedys into Paris were so intense that I can

In Paris, crowds mobbed the Kennedys (top). Jackie's clothes, particularly her pillbox hats,
caused a flurry in the fashion world and her mastery of French language and culture visibly charmed
the usually reserved de Gaulle (inset).

feel the excitement again in writing these words. I hung over the balcony of the Quai d'Orsai, the government guest palace, and watched the colorful parade wending its way around the Place de la Concorde and over the bridge to the Left Bank, with thousands of screaming Parisians lining the route. President de Gaulle had given the people a holiday, and it seemed as though the entire country had shown up.

People fainted in the crush, and the sounds of ambulance sirens mingled with the roar of fighter jets flying overhead in a formation salute. The noise was deafening. *"Tout pour l'Amérique!"* ("All this for America!") commented a *fonctionnaire* of the French government who shared the balcony with me. The cries of *"Vive l'Amérique!"* rang out from tongues that spoke many languages. And through it all, the constant chant of "Jacqu-ie! Jacqu-ie!"

Our final evening in Paris, General and Madame de Gaulle hosted a good-bye banquet at the Palace of Versailles. As schoolgirls Jackie and I had toured the chateau and dreamed about what it would have been like to be a member of the court of the Sun King, Louis XIV. The farewell dinner was held in the Hall of Mirrors, at a long, rectangular table set with exquisite porcelain, crystal, and silver. Eighteenth-century vermeil candelabra held long white tapers that cast a warm glow on the newly restored ceiling frescoes and on the white lace tablecloth visible beneath the centerpieces of peach-colored flowers.

We dined on six courses accompanied by three wines and a champagne, with the serving staff appearing miraculously and almost silently from behind massive, eighteenth-century painted screens, which concealed the serving tables, electricity

generators, warming ovens, and ice coolers. I remember thinking the whole thing was a logistical miracle, carried off with the style and panache for which the French are so renowned.

As if the dinner was not memorable enough, the after-dinner entertainment provided a sublime historical exclamation point. Toward us through the darkened corridors of the palace came a group of musicians dressed in the costumes of the eighteenth century and playing period instruments. Surrounded by liveried footmen lighting our way with burning candelabra, we walked down long hallways to the palace's recently restored jewel of a theater. There, seated on tiny chairs fit for eighteenth-century legs and posteriors, not twentieth-century ones, we watched a ballet commissioned for Louis XV, with torches as spotlights, performed just as it would have been for the King. It was magic.

Going home that night, our motorcade passed slowly through the gardens of Versailles as the French and American national anthems floated out over the giant trees. The lead limousine, bearing the Kennedys, stopped briefly at an illuminated fountain that shot skyrockets of diamond sprays into the air. JFK and Jackie got out of their car, walked to the fountain, and stood for a few minutes hand in hand, while the rest of us waited respectfully in our vehicles. This special moment was theirs and theirs alone. But we savored it in our own way as much as they. It made all the exhausting, enervating, infuriating months of campaigning worth it. Then they returned to their limo and we moved on as the procession dissolved into the Paris night.

Little did I realize the First Lady would soon have me organizing an evening on almost as complicated, if not as opulent, a scale.

The glittering evening at Versailles began with dinner in the fabled Hall of Mirrors (opposite top). For the first time, electric lights illuminated the ceiling frescoes, to spectacular effect. (Opposite bottom) Jackie wore a bell-skirted Givenchy original as a tribute to French design, and topped it with a regal tiara. (Right) All eyes were on Jackie as a standing ovation greeted the official party in the newly-restored Louis XV theater. In a speech the day before, JFK had wryly introduced himself as "the man who accompanied Jacqueline Kennedy to Paris."

A LUNCHEON
WITH PRINCESS GRACE

MAY 24, 1961

Her Serene Highness turns a gaze of frank admiration on the charismatic President.
(To my staff, her stylish turban looked like a fancy bathing cap!)

IN THE 1960S, PRINCESS GRACE HELD ALMOST THE same fascination for the public as Jacqueline Kennedy. Both of these beautiful first ladies led seemingly fairy-tale lives; both had married handsome older men; both had named a daughter Caroline. So naturally the White House staff was buzzing with excitement when we learned the former movie star and her dashing prince would be the guests of honor at a small, informal luncheon with the Kennedys and a few guests.

The setting would be rather different from Princess Grace's first meeting with JFK which had been in a hospital room. In the fall of 1954, Grace Kelly had met Jackie at a New York dinner party. The then Senator Kennedy was in the hospital recovering from painful back surgery, and Jackie had persuaded the classically beautiful actress to accompany her and her sister to the hospital to help cheer him up. They asked her to pretend she was the new night nurse, and after much coaxing, she agreed. Grace shyly entered his room and introduced herself. JFK, of course, recognized her at once. It had long been rumored that Jack Kennedy and Grace Kelly had nurtured crushes on each other. Knowing the President, he probably enjoyed his wife's natural reaction of jealousy to Grace, and knowing Jackie, I suspect that she got Grace into a nurse's uniform so the actress would not look nearly as smashing as she did in her French designer original.

A beaming Princess Grace and Prince Rainier are clearly pleased to be visiting the new occupants of the White House.

In a 1965 interview with Paul Gallico for the archives of the Kennedy Library, Princess Grace remembered the hospital prank and also recalled the White House luncheon fondly, particularly one conversation with the President:

"He turned to me suddenly and asked: 'Is that a Givenchy you're wearing?' The astonishing thing was that day, *that* particular dress just happened to be one.

"I said, 'How clever of you, Mr. President! How ever did you know?'

"'Oh,' he replied, 'I'm getting pretty good at it — now that fashion is becoming more important than politics and the press is paying more attention to Jackie's clothes than to my speeches.'"

(Personally, I think this was a lucky guess on JFK's part, since he knew nothing about haute couture except to complain about its cost!)

Joining the Prince and Princess at the luncheon were several other guests, including Mr. and Mrs. Fred Coe. A well-known director and producer, Fred Coe had been the President's television adviser during the campaign and had given Grace Kelly a starring role in her first TV drama. During a tour of the house after the meal, both the producer and the former actress were intrigued by the Lincoln Room, since the television play had been about the young Lincoln.

I thought everything about the luncheon had gone extremely well until I saw the President in the

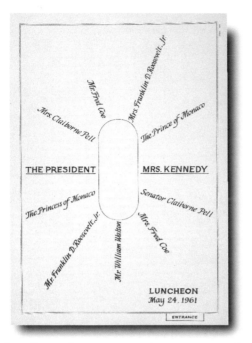

As for all state functions, an elegant seating plan for this luncheon was prepared by White House calligrapher, Sanford Fox.

❧

hallway after the royal couple had left. Throughout the preparations, I had jokingly referred to Prince Rainier as "Prince Reindeer" in all my conversations with the President, and in my memos, too. When he caught up to me, the President was laughing. He said, "For heaven's sake, Tish, don't do that to me again."

"What?"

"Repeatedly call someone like Prince Rainier 'Prince Reindeer,' because at one point at today's lunch I turned to him and addressed him as Prince Reindeer!"

Behind the famous smile, there was a touch of anger, and I didn't blame him. I still had a lot to learn.

A LUNCHEON WITH PRINCESS GRACE

❧

Tender, succulent lamb and freshly picked strawberries are associated with spring in cuisines the world over, and I designed this menu with a warm May afternoon in mind. It was touching to learn that Princess Grace, in her interview with Paul Gallico four years after the event, was able to recall exactly the dishes she had eaten at luncheon that day.

— René Verdon

MENU

SOFT-SHELL CRAB AMANDINE
Puligny-Montrachet 1958

SPRING LAMB À LA BROCHE AUX PRIMEURS
Château Corton Grancey 1955

SALADE MIMOSA
Dom Pérignon 1952

STRAWBERRIES ROMANOFF

PETITS FOURS SECS*

DEMI-TASSES
* recipe page 65

SOFT-SHELL CRAB AMANDINE

*12 soft-shell crabs
(each 2 to 4 inches
in diameter)
or jumbo shrimp*

*1/2 cup
all-purpose flour*

*3/4 tsp each
salt and pepper*

*1/3 cup
vegetable oil*

2 tbsp brandy

2 tbsp butter

1 cup sliced almonds

*1/4 cup
matchstick-length
chopped chives*

*Soft-shell
crab is best
served
simply, and
sautéeing is
ideal, since
it gives the
shell a nice
crispness.*

• Clean crabs, using poultry shears or sharp knife to cut away eyes and mouth. Fold back one side of top shell to expose gills; pull away and discard gills. Turn crab over and fold back tail flap; pull to remove.

• In large bowl, toss crabs with flour, salt, and pepper until evenly coated.

• In large deep skillet, heat half the oil over medium-high heat. Add only enough crabs to cover bottom of pan; cook, shaking skillet gently, for 5 to 10 seconds. Cover pan and cook for 3 minutes; turn crabs, cover, and cook for 3 minutes longer or until crabs are browned but not scorched. Transfer to paper towel-lined tray and pat gently to remove excess oil. Place on ovenproof platter in 200°F oven to keep warm.

• Clean skillet with paper towel and return to heat; in remaining oil, cook remaining crabs. Add to platter in oven. Add brandy to skillet; cook, stirring to scrape up any brown bits, for 30 seconds. Drizzle over crabs.

• Meanwhile, in another skillet, heat butter over medium-high heat until beginning to brown. Stir in the almonds; cook, stirring, for 1 to 2 minutes or until golden. Using slotted spoon, remove almonds and scatter over crabs; drizzle with brown butter. Sprinkle with chopped chives. Makes 6 appetizer servings.

*Monaco's royal
couple are
greeted by the
Kennedys (left)
and meet the
press (right).*

SPRING LAMB À LA BROCHE AUX PRIMEURS

1 ¹/₂ lb lean lamb loin

¹/₄ cup olive oil

2 tbsp each chopped fresh rosemary and parsley

1 clove garlic, minced

¹/₂ tsp each salt and pepper

¹/₄ cup mint jelly, melted

SPRING VEGETABLES:

12 each baby carrots, tiny turnips, small new red potatoes, and pearl onions

1 tbsp butter

1 cup chicken stock

1 bay leaf

¹/₄ tsp each salt and pepper

18 French beans (haricots verts), stem end removed

1 cup fresh peas

¹/₄ cup dry sherry

I suggest serving the meat on a skewer with a garnish of oven-braised spring vegetables for a colorful main course.

• Place 6 long wooden skewers in water to soak for 15 minutes.

• Meanwhile, using sharp knife, trim visible fat and gristle from lamb; cut trimmed lamb into 1-inch cubes. In large bowl, stir together olive oil, rosemary, parsley, garlic, salt, and pepper. Add lamb and toss to combine.

• Remove skewers from water and pat dry. Thread equal amounts of cubed meat onto each skewer. Reserve any remaining marinade. (Lamb can be covered and refrigerated for up to 24 hours; bring to room temperature for 30 minutes before proceeding.)

• SPRING VEGETABLES: Cut carrots, turnips, and potatoes into long, thin olive shapes, leaving one side covered in skin. (Alternatively, vegetables can be quartered.) Peel pearl onions. Reserve.

• In deep, heavy skillet, melt butter with chicken stock over medium-high heat. Bring to boil; stir in bay leaf, salt, and pepper. Stir onions into hot stock mixture; reduce heat to medium-low and simmer for 5 minutes. Stir in carrots, turnips, and potatoes; cover and cook for about 20 minutes, or until vegetables are tender but still firm. Stir in beans and peas; cook for 5 minutes.

• Using slotted spoon, remove vegetables from liquid and place on heated platter; tent with foil and reserve. Bring liquid to boil over medium-high heat; boil for 2 minutes or until thickened and glossy. Stir in sherry; boil for 2 to 3 minutes or until reduced to glaze. Stir in vegetables and toss to coat; cook for 2 minutes, turning often, until well coated. Taste and adjust seasoning, if necessary.

• Meanwhile, place reserved lamb on lightly greased broiling pan in top third of oven; broil, turning often and basting with any remaining marinade, for 8 to 10 minutes or until meat begins to brown. Brush with mint jelly and broil for 3 minutes longer or until cooked to medium-rare. Remove to warmed platter; tent with foil and keep warm.

• To serve, divide vegetables among 6 plates. Top each with 1 kabob. Makes 6 servings.

SALADE MIMOSA

∞

• I lightened up this French classic by turning it into a green salad dressed in a light olive-oil-and-wine-vinegar dressing, tossed with finely chopped hard-cooked egg yolk.

STRAWBERRIES ROMANOFF

∞

1 cup vanilla ice cream

4 cups halved small strawberries

2 tbsp each curaçao and Grand Marnier or other orange-flavored liqueur

1/2 cup whipping cream

1 tbsp confectioner's sugar

1/2 tsp pure vanilla extract

Candied violets or mint leaves

• Place ice cream in refrigerator for 30 minutes or until soft enough to smooth easily with the back of spoon.

• Meanwhile, place strawberries in large bowl. Pour curaçao and Grand Marnier over berries; stir gently to combine. Let stand for 30 minutes.

• In large chilled bowl and using electric mixer, beat whipping cream at low speed for 45 seconds or until slightly thickened. Add sugar and vanilla; increase speed to medium-high and beat for 3 minutes, or until thick.

• In large bowl, stir softened ice cream with wooden spoon until soft. Using rubber spatula, fold dollop of whipped cream into ice cream. Add remaining whipped cream and fold gently until well combined.

• Into each of 6 chilled glass dessert bowls, spoon enough strawberries to just cover bottom; top with large dollop of cream mixture, then divide remaining berries, and any juices, among bowls. Distribute remaining cream equally. Garnish each dish with candied violets or mint leaves. Serve immediately. Makes 6 servings.

TIPS:
• *If strawberries are large, cut into quarters.*
• *Candied violets can be purchased at most upscale grocers or cake decorating shops. If you make your own — by lightly spraying petals with Simple Syrup (see recipe page 78) and dredging in extra-fine sugar — be sure to use only organically grown violets and serve within two days.*

This dish was first made in honor of the Russian Imperial family. I customized this classic by folding whipped cream into softened ice cream to make a cool, light-tasting version.

A CANDLELIT DINNER
AT MOUNT VERNON

JULY 11, 1961

"Cecil Wall, the resident director, telephoned to say that Mount Vernon would be at your disposal any evening this spring or summer from 5:30 on for a private party. He said that it is fabulous in the early evening with the setting sun and the beauty of the river. The public is kept out after five and they could manage to have a caterer serve a supper. The rooms of the house are thrown open as though it were being lived in. You might want to keep this in mind for a little special entertaining of special pals."

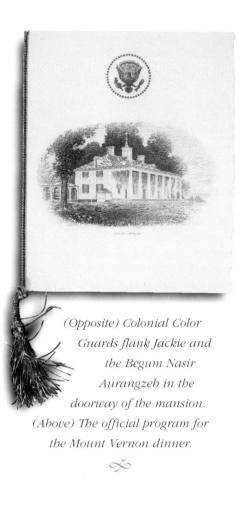

(Opposite) Colonial Color Guards flank Jackie and the Begum Nasir Aurangzeb in the doorway of the mansion. (Above) The official program for the Mount Vernon dinner.

WHEN I WROTE THIS short memo to Jackie, I thought George Washington's stately home would be a suitable setting for a small party inside the mansion. Only in those wonderful years could "a little special entertaining of special pals" turn into an exquisite alfresco state dinner and concert for 132 guests!

A state dinner had never before been held outside the White House, let alone on a lawn sloping down to the Potomac. The Kennedys, however, had loved the splendid dinner given in their honor at Versailles earlier that year, and an invitation to use one of their own country's most revered historic sites as the location for a party held obvious appeal. Within a few days of receiving my note, Jackie set in motion a plan so ambitious that one of the military aides compared it to the logistics required for a full-scale military engagement.

Like all such White House plans, its initial steps were carried out in great secrecy. There was little point in announcing a state dinner at Mount Vernon if the site was unsuitable, so six of us — J.B. West; Pam Turnure; Anne Lincoln; the President's naval aide, Captain Tazewell Shepard, his Air Force aide, General Godfrey McHugh; and I — joined Jackie for a clandestine meeting at Mount Vernon. Accompanied by Cecil Wall and Mrs. Francis F. Beirne, the regent of the Mount Vernon Ladies' Association, we toured the building and grounds, trying to pose as a group of ordinary tourists. It didn't work. The press kept close tabs on Mrs. Kennedy, and that day was no exception. Our ruse was uncovered within minutes, forcing us to conduct our conversations in whispers for the rest of the afternoon.

What we found was daunting, to say the least. I was accustomed to planning events where at least the basic amenities were provided, but Washington's house resembled an Adirondack camp in all but appearance — virtually no electricity, no heating, and limited rest-room and kitchen facilities. The last time it had been used for an official function was in 1926, when a small luncheon had been held there for Queen Marie of Rumania. That the house had been used infrequently for entertaining seemed perfectly understandable to me, given its obvious drawbacks, but one look at Jackie's animated face and I knew we were all doomed. Enchanted by our founding father's home, she was determined to show it off to her fellow Americans and the world. Where the rest of us saw insurmountable problems, she saw possibilities. She peppered our hosts with questions in that soft-spoken, charming way of hers: Can we bring in our own refrigeration equipment? What about bathroom facilities and parking? It would be simpler, wouldn't it, to serve the meal outside? Is there a flat enough area on the lawn to put up tables under a tent — a very beautiful tent, that is? Our surprised hosts promised to consult their board of regents. But when they did, later that week, many of the vice-regents were appalled at the thought of a hundred people merrily eating and drinking on the sacred grounds. Fortunately, Mrs. Beirne, who had a sense of history, won them over, and we began to plan one of the most memorable evenings of the Kennedy years in the White House.

One upcoming state visit, in early July, was that of the President of Pakistan, General Ayub Khan. During those Cold War years, Pakistan had become an important ally of the United States, and it was decided that their President would be offered a state dinner at Mount Vernon on July 11. This left us only four short weeks to devise and carry out a battle plan — scarcely enough time for planning a simple dinner at the White House, let alone one in which every single item had to be transported to the site of the party. If the delightful Mr. Wall

had known the armies we would be unleashing on his quiet historic site, I'm sure he would have promptly pulled in the welcome mat.

Deciding what to serve and how to serve it was the first item on our checklist. René Verdon and Jackie met several times to discuss the menu. It would be French cuisine, *naturellement*, but Jackie wanted it to have overtones of the meals Martha Washington served her guests. Because the Kennedys' visitors were Muslims, no wine could be used in the cooking. This restriction presented no difficulties for our talented chef, but after its preparation in the White House kitchen, the meal would have to be transported along the Memorial Parkway by Army field kitchen trucks, unloaded, assembled in a tent, and served outside! After much thought, René presented Jackie with a simple but elegant menu, assuring her that "this food will travel well." He had wisely chosen a main dish that would improve in flavor upon standing and side dishes that took very little time to assemble.

Jackie suggested a marquee be erected over round tables on the lawn, "then if there is a light shower — we can stand on the piazza and go quickly under [the] tent — a striped one — a gray & white would be nice." For the tables, which would each seat eight, she requested "yellow cloths if we have enough — otherwise white — and . . . small vermeil cachepots (Pres. adores such) with mixed freesia or whatever is in season — not daisies in middle — Can we use vermeil knives, forks, plates from the White House . . . ? "

Although the President didn't usually bother with such details, in this case he also dashed off a memo: "See that they have all the Lowestoft bowls in house filled with flowers — very low — ask

Dinner

AVOCADO AND CRABMEAT MIMOSA

Haut-Brion Blanc
1958

POULET CHASSEUR
COURONNE DE RIZ CLAMART

Moet et Chandon
Imperial Brut
1955

FRAMBOISES À LA CRÈME CHANTILLY
PETITS-FOURS SECS

DEMI-TASSE AND LIQUEURS

Mount Vernon, Virginia
July 11, 1961

While the elegant marquee on Mount Vernon's lawn (above) was decorated with garlands of flowers, René Verdon and his staff worked on last-minute meal preparations in a separate kitchen tent.

Mr. West to ask Mr. Pecora [Mrs. Paul Mellon's horticultural expert] for suggestions."

The next item on our formidable and ever-lengthening list was transportation. In addition to trucking generators, tables, chairs, china, linen, crystal, food, and White House staff, including twenty-two butlers, to Mount Vernon, we had to arrange to take the guests there by boat. Not surprisingly, this was JFK's idea. A PT boat, two presidential yachts, and a Navy yacht were pressed into service for the leisurely cruise from the Naval Weapons Plant in downtown Washington up the Potomac to the

(Above) The President's yacht, the Honey Fitz, *carried JFK, Ayub Khan and one group of guests from the Washington docks to the foot of Mount Vernon. (Below) Headscarves were required for Pam Turnure, right, and me, left, on a practice run up the Potomac.*

Mount Vernon pier. Several practice runs were made in the weeks leading up to the dinner, and during them we discovered that even on a muggy evening, it could be overly breezy and cool out on the water. To ensure that the female guests did not arrive chilled to the bone or with their hair in tangled clumps, we rounded up as many sweaters and chiffon scarves as we could find among ourselves and placed them onboard each vessel. (They were a delightful hodgepodge of French designer things lent by Jackie, and items from Bloomingdale's and Macy's lent by the rest of us.)

(Right) By late afternoon, we were putting the finishing touches on the dinner preparations. (Above) The dining tables reflected the delicate blue and yellow color scheme of the marquee.

As July approached, my binder grew thicker and thicker with Jackie's distinctive memos written on yellow legal pads, information and queries from other staff members, and my own copious notes. Would we ever be able to cover all the remaining details before the eleventh? Even the invitations weren't a simple matter. Each envelope contained six inserts, including a map of the Naval Weapons Plant and pier and admission cards for cars and vessels. As those around her doubted that we could pull it off, Jackie remained serene and confident in her staff's abilities. Her innate control of endless details and superb sense of organization were accompanied by a quiet little phrase of iron, "*Of course* it can be done."

By the day of the dress rehearsal, forty-eight hours before the dinner, myriad items — from arranging the building of a wooden bandstand for the National Symphony Orchestra's after-dinner performance to borrowing portable toilets — had been ticked off the list. It had been a hectic four weeks and a mammoth undertaking, one that was later misguidedly criticized for its expense. But as Pierre Salinger, the President's press secretary, told reporters after the event, "This dinner was carried out under a plan which has been initiated by Mrs. Kennedy since she has been in the White House and a substantial — in fact the bulk of — the special items for the dinner were donated by public-spirited citizens as a way of helping the White House in extending welcome to President Ayub Khan."

Quite frankly, cost was not uppermost in my mind at the time. The weather was. I had every member of my staff and an entire convent praying for a sunny day. The weather bureau was being cagey, promising neither fair weather nor foul.

Heavy rain — blowing in on the diners under the marquee, requiring the cancellation of the after-dinner concert on the lawn, or, indeed, of the entire event — was something none of us wanted to contemplate.

The only mishap of the dress rehearsal happened as a group of us, pretending to be the presidential party, were slowly driven up the narrow road from the Mount Vernon dock to the house. As our limousines passed between two rows of Marines standing at parade attention, I heard a strange crunching noise. It turned out to be the sound of the cars running over several highly polished boots! Not a word was heard from any of the young soldiers, just the peculiar sound of their heavy boots being crushed. Although this didn't seem to be a minor mishap to me, their colonel assured me that his men were uninjured. Besides, he said, they were Marines, certainly able to withstand more than the odd tire running over their feet. Nevertheless, for the safety of his men and my own peace of mind, I asked him to withdraw the Marines from one side of the road to give the cars — and the soldiers' boots — plenty of room.

The day before the dinner, the decorations for the marquee arrived. The thirty-by-fifty-foot tent, which was blue on top and buttercup yellow inside, had been erected earlier in the week by Philadelphia tent maker John L. Vanderherchen. My former cohort from Tiffany's, Gene Moore, the famous window designer, graciously volunteered his services to decorate it. He created a summer wonderland using garlands of smilax, white and yellow ribbons, and, of course, flowers. Mrs. Paul Mellon's gardener had appeared at noon with asters, baby's breath, blue delphiniums, yellow

carnations, lemon lilies and blue bachelor's buttons for the centerpieces. Their bright colors complemented the blue cushions on the delicate black iron chairs and the yellow tablecloths on the sixteen round tables. A canopied walkway was built, connecting the dining tent with the tent from which the food would be served. Meanwhile, the bandstand for the post-dinner concert was being constructed on the opposite side of the lawns from the dining area. Workmen were still hammering away on it as I left for home that day.

And, to my alarm, they were still putting it together when I arrived in the early afternoon of July 11. If this weren't enough to worry about, a steady stream of military buses and trucks began roaring up the driveway. They carried supplies and the soldiers who would be performing the military drill at the party, helping on various work details, or standing guard around the perimeter of the two-hundred-acre site. Soon the country air was filled with exhaust fumes and the clamor of young men changing into their dress uniforms behind shrubbery, hauling portable toilets into place, and spraying the freshly mown grass for bugs. I added my own voice to the racket, finding myself ordering full colonels to move the Army vehicles out of sight and directing their subordinates to hide the ugly eight-holer toilets behind trees or bushes.

After we spent an hour carefully camouflaging the portable toilets and spraying them mightily with room fragrance (an act of futility), someone reported poison ivy in the area we had selected. Mr. Wall assured me that a noxious weed would not be permitted to grow on the estate of the father of our country. In my more-than-slightly panicky state, I of course quickly agreed with him.

NATIONAL SYMPHONY ORCHESTRA

Tonight the National Symphony performs for the second State occasion this year, having been invited to present the Inaugural Concert for President Kennedy, January 19, 1961.

The Orchestra was founded in 1931 and has taken its place among the great symphonic ensembles in the world, under the leadership of Music Director Howard Mitchell. The National Symphony has also been a musical envoy for the United States, having recently toured Central and South America under the auspices of the President's Special International Program for Cultural Presentations.

Mr. Lloyd Geisler, Associate Conductor, will conduct the Orchestra this evening in the absence of Mr. Mitchell.

NATIONAL SYMPHONY ORCHESTRA

Program

Mr. Lloyd Geisler, *Conducting*

GOULD . . . . "American Salute"

MOZART . . . . Allegro con spirito from Symphony No. 35 in D Major, "Haffner"

DEBUSSY . . . . . Dialogue Between the Wind and the Sea from "La Mer"

GERSHWIN . . . ."American in Paris"

An outdoor concert by the National Symphony Orchestra was to be the after-dinner entertainment, but erecting a wooden bandshell and ensuring proper acoustics would prove challenging.

Just as everything seemed to be falling into place, disaster struck. Our prayers had been answered weatherwise, but three hours before the guests were to arrive, the conductor from the National Symphony Orchestra cheerfully announced that with the orchestra in its present location nobody would be able to hear the concert. I thought he must be exaggerating, but when J.B. West and I went to investigate, it was true. The wooded ravine behind the recently completed bandstand seemed to suck the sound down into it. The head of the National Parks Service who was standing nearby said firmly, "The orchestra will play because we will fix the problem." Then he and his carpenters threw themselves into erecting an acoustical shell behind the stage, no doubt whipped into a frenzy by our informing them that the entire prestige of the United States of America rested squarely on their shoulders. The hammering resumed — and the insects returned.

By four o'clock, the mosquitoes were holding their own state dinner. The sprayers were ordered back to work, and, as luck would have it, the spray began drifting toward the kitchen tent where the food had just arrived from the White House. René

"The mint juleps, in their silver-frosted cups, were served on the piazza and on the broad lawn overlooking the river Washington had so much loved."

— Mary van Rensselaer Thayer

began worrying that everyone would die of insecticide poisoning. At that point, all of us were punch-drunk with fatigue, and two brave Secret Servicemen volunteered to test the food to quell our chef's fears. They pronounced it delicious, with no chemical

aftertaste and they did not expire — so the meal preparations continued.

While these last-minute details were being worked out at Mount Vernon, the guests were being piped aboard the four boats by the Navy at the Naval Weapons Plant in Washington. Each female guest was escorted to her ship by a formally attired White House aide. Once onboard, the passengers were served cocktails and hors d'oeuvres and entertained by small Marine band units or, in the case of the *Sequoia*, a trio from the Lester Lanin orchestra. The flotilla got under way ahead of schedule, the

last vessel leaving at six twenty-five. As the Kennedys and their guests leisurely cruised upriver, they retraced the journey made by many of George Washington's guests to his home, although in considerably greater comfort. They were greeted at the Mount Vernon pier with a military salute and then shepherded into the waiting limousines for the uneventful ride to the house. This time, as each car passed, the Marines were able to execute a rippling salute with their guns without fear of their toes being crushed. On a whim, one small group of guests, led by the athletic Bobby and Ethel Kennedy, decided to ignore the proffered ride and hike up the steep, twisty road to the mansion, in spite of their evening attire.

On their arrival, the senators, representatives, Pakistani officials, and Kennedy friends and family members attending the party could tour Washington's home, where he had lived for forty-five years, before proceeding to the colonnaded veranda overlooking the Potomac. There they were served bourbon mint juleps in sterling silver cups (just as George Washington used to do) or frosted orange drinks for the Muslim guests. Once all of the guests were assembled, President and Mrs. Kennedy led President Ayub Khan and his daughter, the Begum Nasir Aurangzeb, to the other side of the mansion, where a military drill was to take place. The Kennedys

After a tour of Washington's home (opposite) the Kennedys and their guests observed a re-enactment of a Revolutionary War-era military drill.

particularly enjoyed these colorful pageants, and they knew their guest, a general, would, too. For this occasion, fifty-four Marines lined the drive carrying flags of the states and territories. The Army's Colonial Color Guard and Fife and Drum Corps, costumed in the scarlet coats, powdered wigs, and tricornered hats of the Continental Army, performed the same drill their forefathers had in 1776.

At the end of the dramatic drill, the President's Own, as this red-coated corps has been affectionately called since Washington's time, aimed their muskets and fired a smoky barrage of blanks at an unexpected target. Although we had rehearsed the drill, we had not taken into account the position of the sixty-strong press corps, who, as it happened, stood directly in the line of fire. As the deafening roar subsided, a *New York Times* reporter in the stunned group waved his white handkerchief in surrender. Both Chiefs of State and their guests broke into uncontrolled laughter. Later I overheard a reporter tell President Kennedy, "That's no way to solve your press problems, Mr. President. Total annihilation won't do it."

After the military pageant, at eight-thirty, the presidential party formed a receiving line on the piazza, where Washington had spent many warm summer evenings just like this one gazing over a view that he considered unrivaled by any other in North America. As the guests strolled into dinner, out on the river the lights of the Coast Guard patrol boats crisscrossed the dark water, while inside the tent white candles in hurricane lanterns placed on every table cast a soft light on the huge wheels of huckleberry and water oak that encircled the center tent poles. As they walked with their escorts across the lawn from the veranda, the women looked from a distance like pale butterflies. A light breeze fluttered the pastel-colored organza, chiffon, and lace of their dresses. Each of us who entered the beautifully decorated marquee that night could not help but feel part of a very special event. As René's wonderful meal was served, the dining area sparkled. Candlelight flashed off diamond earrings and necklaces, and glimmered on the crystal goblets and vermeil flatware. Even a group of fireflies appeared to add their special glow to the evening.

Presiding over her guests was a radiant First Lady in a sleeveless white organza and lace evening gown, sashed at the waist in chartreuse silk. President Ayub Khan's daughter, dressed in a sumptuous silk sari, sat on the President's right. Mrs. Kennedy's sisters-in-law also wore white dresses with colored sashes, while the President and his male relatives were attired in smart black tuxedoes.

Throughout the dinner, the Air Force Strolling Strings, playing romantic ballads on their violins, wandered among the tables and serenaded the guests. Music ended the evening, as well. After dessert and coffee, we walked along a path lit by burning citronella candles to the concert area, where the seventy-four-piece National Symphony Orchestra performed brilliantly, its acoustical shell now in perfect working order. Around our hastily constructed and reconstructed stage, floodlights had been used to silhouette clusters of trees — trees Washington himself had helped to plant. Champagne was served throughout the performance of "American Salute" by Morton Gould, the Allegro con spirito from Mozart's Symphony no. 35 in D Major, Debussy's "Dialogue between the Wind and the Sea" from *La Mer*, and George Gershwin's "American in Paris." The exuberant music and the historic surroundings cast a spell over the audience, and as the encore — "The Rakoczy March" by Liszt — drew to a close, President Kennedy jumped to his feet to congratulate the conductor, Lloyd Geisler. It was a jubilant ending to a magical evening.

Afterward, I wondered if our official guests realized how much work and planning had gone into this dinner, and if they realized how greatly they had been honored. I think they must have. People left Washington's estate quietly, perhaps in awe of what they had experienced. President Kennedy put his arm around his wife as they took one last look at the house, then entered their limo. They must have been saying to each other, "A job well done." When you stop to consider what could have gone wrong, but didn't, perhaps George and Martha Washington really were helping us out from their special places in heaven.

Each of the sixteen round tables was covered with a pale yellow cloth and lit with candles in hurricane lamps. (Top left) At one table, Ayub Khan's daughter sat between President Kennedy and Franklin D. Roosevelt Jr. Theodore Roosevelt's daughter, Alice Longworth, is seen on the far right. Jackie entertained the Pakistani president (bottom left) at another table. Attorney-General Robert Kennedy (above) also acted as a host.

At Mount Vernon Jackie wore a sleeveless Oleg Cassini dress made of rows of white lace on white organza,
while the Begum Nasir Aurangzeb shimmered in a white silk sari.

A CANDLELIT DINNER AT MOUNT VERNON

∞

Because this meal had to be prepared at the White House and then transported to Mount Vernon, it is an ideal make-ahead dinner for the home chef. The Petits Fours Secs, a classic palmier cookie in a chocolate coating, can be made the day before, and the Avocado and Crabmeat Mimosa salad can be prepared a few hours ahead. It is worth noting that George Washington also served mint juleps to his guests, an example of the special little touches that made the Kennedys' state dinners so unforgettable.

— René Verdon

Dinner

AVOCADO AND CRABMEAT MIMOSA

Haut-Brion Blanc
1058

POULET CHASSEUR
COURONNE DE RIZ CLAMART

Moet et Chandon
Imperial Brut
1055

FRAMBOISES À LA CRÈME CHANTILLY
PETITS-FOURS SECS

DEMI-TASSE AND LIQUEURS

Mount Vernon, Virginia
July 11, 1961

GEORGE WASHINGTON'S MINT JULEP

∞

1/2 cup lightly packed fresh young mint leaves

1 cup bourbon whiskey

1/3 cup Simple Syrup (recipe, page 78)

3/4 tsp angostura bitters

Confectioner's sugar

Crushed ice

Mint sprigs

• Chill 6 silver cups or heavy cut-glass tumblers on ice in freezer until very cold.

• Meanwhile, in pitcher, stir together mint leaves, bourbon, Simple Syrup, and bitters.

• Dip rim of each cup in confectioner's sugar. Being careful not to disturb sugar frosting, fill each cup two-thirds full with crushed ice. Pour equal amounts of bourbon mixture over ice; add mint sprig to each cup and stir.

• To serve, fill deep tray or julep stand with crushed ice and nestle cups in ice. Makes 6 servings.

This modern version of the Southern classic was served in silver cups on the portico at Mount Vernon. Fruit drinks were provided for our Muslim guests.

AVOCADO AND CRABMEAT MIMOSA

Although the term mimosa is sometimes used to describe an orange garnish, in French cooking it most commonly indicates a recipe that contains chopped egg and watercress.

2 ripe avocados	2 tbsp chili sauce	8 oz cooked fresh crabmeat (or one 7-oz can crab flakes)
1 green onion, minced	1 tbsp prepared horseradish	
2 tsp lemon juice	1/2 tsp Worcestershire sauce	2 cups watercress
Salt		2 hard-cooked egg yolks
Dash hot pepper sauce	White pepper	1 tbsp chopped fresh parsley
3/4 cup mayonnaise		

• Peel half of one avocado. In bowl, mash avocado; add green onion, half of the lemon juice, 1/4 tsp salt, and hot pepper sauce. Stir until well combined. Reserve.

• In separate bowl, stir together mayonnaise, chili sauce, horseradish, Worcestershire sauce, and remaining lemon juice; season to taste with salt and white pepper. Reserve.

• In large bowl, peel remaining 1 1/2 avocados; cut into 1/2-inch cubes. Squeeze excess moisture from crab. Add to cubed avocado and gently combine. Fold in mayonnaise mixture until crab and avocado are evenly coated.

• Line bottoms of 6 chilled open champagne glasses or small glass serving dishes with watercress. Divide crab mixture evenly among glasses; top with dollop of mashed avocado mixture.

• Press egg yolks through fine-mesh sieve; combine with parsley. Sprinkle yolk mixture evenly over each portion. (Mimosas can be covered and refrigerated for up to 3 hours.) Makes 6 servings.

THE KENNEDY STEMWARE

Jackie was so affected by the poverty she saw while campaigning in West Virginia in 1960, that after the election she looked for ways to help the state. In 1961, she commissioned the Morgantown Glassware Guild to produce the White House crystal. Shown here are wineglasses, a tulip champagne glass, a fingerbowl and goblet similar to those used at the Mount Vernon dinner. This same elegant pattern was purchased by many Americans once it became known as "The President's House" crystal.

POULET CHASSEUR

¹/₃ cup all-purpose flour

1 tbsp chopped fresh tarragon

1 tsp chopped fresh thyme

¹/₂ tsp each salt and pepper

6 boneless, skinless chicken breasts

1 egg, beaten

3 tbsp each vegetable oil and butter

¹/₄ cup finely chopped shallots

1 clove garlic, minced

2 cups tiny mushroom caps

2 tomatoes, peeled, seeded and chopped

¹/₂ cup white wine or chicken stock

1 ¹/₄ cups chicken stock

2 tsp tomato paste

Pinch granulated sugar

• In sturdy plastic bag, shake together flour, half the tarragon, thyme, salt, and pepper. Dip chicken, one piece at a time, into egg; dredge in flour mixture.

• In large deep skillet, heat half the oil and butter over medium-high heat. Cook chicken, turning once, for 6 to 8 minutes or until golden brown on both sides. Remove from skillet and keep warm.

• Reduce heat to medium; add remaining oil and butter to skillet. Stir in shallots, garlic, and remaining tarragon; cook, stirring often, for about 5 minutes or until shallots are translucent. Increase heat to medium-high and add mushrooms; cook, stirring often, for 5 minutes or until mushrooms are well browned. Add tomatoes; cook, stirring, for 1 minute.

• Add wine; cook, stirring to scrape up any brown bits, for 1 minute or until liquid is almost evaporated. Stir in stock, tomato paste, and sugar. Boil for 2 minutes or until liquid begins to thicken. Return chicken to pan, turning to coat; cook for 5 minutes or until juices from chicken run clear. Makes 6 servings.

This dish has a classic sauce from the Escoffier era containing mushrooms, shallots, tomatoes and white wine. Because the guests of honor didn't consume alcohol, I used no white wine that evening at Mount Vernon.

"I would rather be at Mount Vernon,

with a friend or two about me, than be attended at the

seat of government by the officers of state and the

representatives of every power in Europe."

— President Kennedy quoting
George Washington in his dinner toast

COURONNE DE RIZ CLAMART

Named for the Hauts-de-Seine district of France, which is famous for its pea production, clamart *is a classic French garnish used to accompany everything from chicken* en cocotte *to scrambled eggs.*

2 tsp butter	1/4 cup freshly grated Parmesan cheese	1 plum tomato, peeled, seeded, and finely chopped
1/2 cup each finely chopped red and green pepper	1 cup chicken or vegetable stock	1/4 tsp each salt and pepper
3 cups cooked long-grain rice	2 tbsp chopped fresh parsley	1 cup baby peas or sweetlets, warmed
2 eggs, beaten		

• In skillet, melt half the butter over medium-high heat. Add peppers; cook, stirring often, for about 5 minutes or until lightly browned. Reserve.

• In bowl, gently stir together rice, eggs, Parmesan cheese, chicken stock, and parsley. Stir in peppers, tomato, salt, and pepper.

• Spoon rice mixture into generously buttered 1 quart round tube mold or Bundt pan, packing down gently with spoon. Bake in 350°F oven for 25 minutes or until lightly browned. Remove from oven and let stand for 2 minutes. Invert serving platter over top of mold and turn out rice mixture. Toss peas with remaining butter; spoon into center of rice ring. Makes 6 servings.

FRAMBOISES À LA CRÈME CHANTILLY

• This simple yet succulent medley of raspberries topped with whipped cream sweetened with sugar and flavored with vanilla combines the freshest of seasonal fruits with a classically rich topping. The name Chantilly is derived from the Chateau of Chantilly, where the renowned chef Vatel earned a glorious culinary reputation during the seventeenth century.

PETITS FOURS SECS

❧

2 cups all-purpose flour	3/4 cup unsalted butter	3/4 cup granulated sugar
1 tsp salt	2/3 cup ice water (approx)	5 oz semisweet chocolate

• In large bowl, sift together flour and salt. Cut butter into 1-inch cubes; add half to flour mixture. Using pastry blender or two knives, cut butter into flour until mixture resembles coarse crumbs. Rub with fingers until broken into fine crumbs. Make well in center of flour mixture; gradually add water, mixing until dough is soft but not sticky.

• On lightly floured surface, roll dough into 6- x 18-inch rectangle. Scatter remaining butter over two-thirds of the dough. Fold unbuttered dough over half of the buttered portion. Fold dough again so butter is completely enclosed in layers of dough; gently press edges closed with fingers. Wrap in plastic wrap and chill for 15 minutes.

• Remove dough from refrigerator; roll into 6- x 18-inch rectangle. Fold in thirds to form 6- x 6-inch square; gently press edges closed. Wrap in plastic wrap and chill for 15 minutes. Repeat entire step.

• Sprinkle lightly floured work surface with sugar; turning pastry frequently to coat both sides with sugar, roll into 12- x 14-inch rectangle. Fold up long ends of pastry to meet in middle. Fold again to meet in middle. Fold ends in a third time so that pastry resembles tightly wrapped scroll.

• Place on plastic-lined baking sheet and wrap well with plastic wrap. Refrigerate for 30 minutes or until firm. Unwrap pastry; using serrated knife, cut into 1/4-inch slices. Place on parchment paper-lined baking sheets; let stand for 15 minutes.

• Bake in 375°F oven for 8 minutes; turn and bake for 8 minutes more or until golden on both sides. Let cool on sheets for 5 minutes; transfer to racks and cool completely.

• Meanwhile, melt chocolate over hot (not boiling) water; dip one end of each cookie in chocolate. Shake off excess chocolate and place on wax paper-lined rack; cool until chocolate is set. Makes about 32 cookies.

TIP: *If your kitchen is warm, chill chocolate-dipped cookies for 2 to 3 minutes to fully set chocolate.*

The name petits fours has come to mean almost any pastry or cake small enough to be eaten in one or two bites. The word sec denotes that these particular petits fours have no cream or icing. Here I present a classic palmier cookie that has been dipped in melted chocolate.

THE NIGHT CASALS PLAYED

NOVEMBER 13, 1961

"The feeling of hospitality, of warmth, of welcome, the taste with which everything
was done, the goodness of everything — it was just good."

— Leonard Bernstein

I F, LIKE JACQUELINE KENNEDY, YOU WERE THE chatelaine of the White House, you could have anyone you desired seated in your dining room. My office had a terrible problem fending off the famous people who tried to get themselves invited for dinner. For some it became an obsession. They stopped at nothing to accomplish their goal, because a White House invitation would define them socially. I told the President one day that a man had offered me a thousand dollars to sneak him and his wife onto a dinner guest list. He laughingly replied that if I managed to hike up the price by several thousand dollars, and if I agreed to split it with him,

he'd let me add the couple to the list.

One man was not only invited to dine with the Kennedys but was also asked to entertain afterward. And he turned down the invitation! Pablo Casals, perhaps the greatest cellist who ever lived, was one of the few people I can recall who did not want to come to dinner at the White House.

Washington lawyer and future Supreme Court Justice Abe Fortas, knowing the Kennedys' interest in promoting the arts, had suggested inviting Casals. The Kennedys liked the idea, and an invitation was soon on its way to Puerto Rico, where the cellist had lived since 1956. Casals politely

(Opposite) Pablo Casals poses
with accompanists Mieczyslaw
Horszowski and Alexander
Schneider after rehearsing the
program for their concert (below).
(Right) The Kennedys with
Governor and Señora Muñoz
Marín of Puerto Rico.

Mr. PABLO CASALS, *Cello*
Mr. Mieczyslaw Horszowski, *Piano*
Mr. Alexander Schneider, *Violin*

Monday, November 13, 1961
THE WHITE HOUSE

*Scarlet-coated members of the
Marine orchestra (left) who had
played before and during the state
dinner could not resist peeking
through a door to the East Room
to hear Casal's performance.
I had been privileged to be the
audience for the rehearsal
(above) the day before.*

refused the invitation, saying that like many artists he was unable to perform after eating a meal. But according to his biographer, H.L. Kirk, Casals was afraid that acceptance of the invitation would give the impression he had forgiven the American government for supporting Generalissimo Francisco Franco in Spain; he had not played in the United States since 1928. The diplomatic solution to the problem was to hold a state dinner in honor of Governor Luis Muñoz Marin of Puerto Rico, a close friend of Casals, and to invite the artist to play for the guests afterward. This would enable Casals, who greatly admired President Kennedy for his world peace efforts, to consider his participation in the evening as private rather than public.

We were all moved when Casals agreed to break his self-imposed exile to come to the White House. But I had perhaps the greatest thrill of all — a private concert. The day before the dinner, Casals, accompanied by pianist Mieczyslaw Horszowski and violinist Alexander Schneider, rehearsed in the East Room. I sat alone on one of the ballroom chairs as the audience. It was three hours of exquisite, almost excruciatingly pure sound. The faces of the two other people in the room, the signal corpsmen recording the music, were transfixed by what they heard coming over their earphones. I had seen them many times before during taping sessions, their expressions placid, even vapid, with an occasional flicker of a facial muscle from chewing gum. That afternoon, from two to five, they were, as I was, totally involved in listening to the extraordinary music produced by those three talented men.

White House Press Secretary Pierre Salinger, who had been a concert pianist for a short time in his youth, was asked by Jackie to draw up a guest list for the dinner. He included on it some of America's top composers: Samuel Barber, Leonard Bernstein, Aaron Copland, Giancarlo Menotti and Virgil Thomson. Well-known conductors such as Eugene Ormandy and Leopold Stokowski were also invited, as well as patrons of the arts and government officials. The list was so large, at 155, that the Blue Room had to be used as well as the State Dining Room, with the President presiding over the eleven tables in the dining room and Mrs. Kennedy over the five tables in the adjoining room.

Both rooms, on that cool fall evening, provided a warm backdrop to the Kennedys' legendary hospitality. Jackie had asked that the fireplaces be lit. In the State Dining Room the artists' wives admired the centerpieces surrounded by candles — white daisies, white and yellow carnations, and orange bouvardia — on pale yellow cloths, while in the Blue Room the tables were covered in blue cloths and adorned with white anemones, blue lace flowers and bachelor's buttons. Their husbands were no doubt oblivious to the decorations, as many men are. Everyone was simply delighted to be there, pleased that the arts were being recognized by the new administration in such a wonderful and historic way.

Leonard Bernstein compared the evening to the last time he had been invited to the White House in another administration, when "the food was ordinary, and the wines were inferior, and you couldn't smoke.... Compare that to the Casals dinner at the White House in November 1961, at which you were served very good drinks first; where there were ashtrays everywhere just inviting you to poison yourself with cigarettes; where the [receiving] line is formed alphabetically; and where, when you do line up, you are in a less querulous mood because you have a drink and a cigarette; where, when the moment comes for you to greet the President and the First Lady, two ravishing people appear in the doorway who couldn't be more charming if they tried, who make you feel utterly welcome, even with a huge gathering.... The food is marvelous, the wines are delicious, there are cigarettes on the table, people are laughing, laughing out loud, telling stories, jokes, enjoying themselves, glad to be there.... You know, I've never seen so many happy artists in my life. It was a joy to watch it."

After dinner the guests entered the East Room for the concert while the Kennedys and Governor and Señora Muñoz Marin walked to the Green Room to greet the music critics who had been invited to hear the performance. On his way into the East Room, Casals took the time to stop and congratulate the Air Force Strolling Strings, who had been playing in the corridor. The hero worship on the violinists' faces was unmistakable. "Very good. Sounds very good," Casals said, shaking hands with M/Sgt. Charles Gronofsky. After some welcoming remarks by President Kennedy, Casals, Schneider, and Horszowski began to play the Mendelssohn Trio no. 1 in D Minor, op. 49. This was followed by two solos accompanied by piano — Adagio and Allegro in A-flat, op. 70, by Schumann and "Concert

Pieces" by Couperin. As the room erupted in applause at the conclusion of the hour-long performance, the eighty-four-year-old artist beamed with delight. He had not given a recital in a long time. The applause was so prolonged that Casals added an encore, "The Song of the Birds," a Catalan folk song from his birthplace.

As I had been at the rehearsal the day before, the audience was captivated by Casals. "The moment Señor Casals drew his bow across the strings, it was with the power and authority he always has had. Despite his age, he has retained complete muscular control, and even in a long, slow bow there was not the least waver at the tip," reported Paul Henry Lang in the *New York Herald Tribune*.

The concert was particularly meaningful for President Theodore Roosevelt's daughter, Alice Longworth. The Kennedys had a sixth sense about historic connections. Casals had last played at the White House in 1904 for her father. "The cello was Father's favorite instrument," she told Paul Hume of the *Washington Post*. "He was not at all musical, but he adored the cello. I think it must have been because of its gorgeous sound. And of course I was there when Casals played. It was two years before I was married, and I probably had my mind on other paths to glory, but you know how you remember something as marvelous as he was." After the concert, Mrs. Longworth joined Casals, his wife, Marta, and several other guests for a private supper in the Red Room with the Kennedys.

As Jackie wrote to Pierre Salinger the next morning, "Last night was an unbelievable dream." And it was.

After a performance that left his audience breathless (top and middle), Casals is congratulated by the President (above). (Opposite) A gracious tribute from the star performer.

THE NIGHT CASALS PLAYED

✄

*Like many other members of the staff that evening, I listened enchanted at the
East Room door as Pablo Casals performed. There was still a small supper to be served
in the Red Room, but by this time the main dinner was over. The galantine we offered
that night was a particularly memorable feature of the meal.*

— René Verdon

DINNER

*Inglenook Pinot
Chardonnay*

*Almaden
Cabernet
Sauvignon*

*Piper-Heidsieck
1953*

Mousse de sole Amiral

Filet de boeuf Montfermeil

*Galantine de faisan au porto
Salade verte*

*Sorbet au Champagne
Pâtisserie*

The White House
Monday, November 13, 1961

*This versatile
dish can be
served hot or
cold, as an
entrée or an
appetizer.
Shrimp shells
and fish stock
are available
at better fish
markets.*

MOUSSE DE SOLE AMIRAL

✄

SAUCE

¼ cup olive oil	2 cups dry white wine	1 bay leaf
8 oz raw shrimp or crayfish shells	4 cups fish stock	3 tbsp cold butter
¼ cup cognac	1 cup water	2 shallots, minced
1 cup finely chopped leeks	2 tbsp tomato paste	½ cup dessert wine or off-dry Riesling
2 carrots, finely chopped	1 tbsp chopped fresh tarragon	2 tbsp whipping cream
4 cloves garlic, minced		Salt and pepper

MOUSSE

1 lb Dover sole fillets	2 egg whites	1 tsp white pepper
4 oz sea scallops, knob-shaped muscle removed	2 tsp salt	2 cups whipping cream

GARNISH

8 jumbo shrimp, cooked and butterflied	2 tbsp crayfish or flying fish roe	8 sprigs parsley or chervil

• SAUCE: In saucepan, heat half the olive oil over high heat. Add shrimp shells; cook for 5 minutes or until pink but not scorched. Stir in cognac; cook, stirring to scrape up any brown bits, for 1 minute or until liquid is reduced to about 2 tbsp.

• Meanwhile in stock pot or Dutch oven, heat remaining oil over medium heat. Add leeks, carrots, and garlic; cook for 5 minutes or until softened. Add shell mixture; stir in wine and bring to boil. Simmer rapidly for 6 to 7 minutes or until liquid is reduced to about 1 cup. Stir in fish stock and water; return to boil. Add tomato paste, tarragon, and bay leaf. Reduce heat and simmer for 25 minutes. Strain through fine-mesh sieve into bowl; reserve liquid. (Strained liquid can be stored in refrigerator for up to 2 days.)

• In large saucepan, melt 1 tbsp butter over medium heat. Add shallots; cook, stirring often, for 5 minutes or until very soft. Increase heat to high and add dessert wine; bring to boil and boil for 3 to 5 minutes or until liquid is reduced by about half. Add reserved liquid; boil for 20 minutes or until reduced to about 1 cup. Reduce heat to low; whisk in cream until well combined. Whisk in remaining butter, bit by bit, until sauce is glossy and slightly thickened. Season to taste with salt and pepper. Keep warm.

• MOUSSE: Place bowl and blade from food processor in refrigerator for 15 minutes or until well chilled. Cut fish and scallops into 3/4-inch cubes. Place in food processor; add egg whites, salt, and pepper and pulse just until smooth. Refrigerate for 30 minutes or until mixture is very cold.

• Meanwhile, beat half the whipping cream until soft peaks form; reserve. Using wooden spoon, gradually add remaining whipping cream to fish mixture, stirring just until combined. Gently fold in whipped cream. In small pot of boiling water or in microwave oven, cook 1 tsp of the fish mixture; taste sample and adjust seasoning level of remaining mixture if necessary. Refrigerate mixture for 30 minutes or until very cold.

• Butter eight 1/2-cup heatproof ramekins; line bottoms with parchment or waxed paper. Fill ramekins with mousse, tapping each gently on counter to remove any air bubbles. Place in large shallow pan; pour enough boiling water into pan to come halfway up sides of ramekins. Cover pan tightly with foil, making several vent holes with point of knife. Bake in 300°F oven for 20 to 25 minutes or until metal skewer inserted in center of mousse comes out clean.

• To serve, invert each mousse onto warmed dinner plate. Cordon sauce around mousse. Crown each mousse with a butterflied shrimp, dollop of roe, and sprig of parsley. Makes 8 appetizers.

The Kennedys did not commission an official state dinner service of their own, but often used the Truman china on ceremonial occasions.

FILET DE BOEUF MONTFERMEIL

SAUCE

2 tbsp vegetable oil	*1 each carrot and celery stalk, chopped*	*1 each bay leaf and sprig rosemary*
¼ cup finely chopped shallots	*1 tbsp tomato paste*	*3 cups beef stock*
1 clove garlic, minced	*½ tsp granulated sugar*	*2 tbsp cold butter, cubed*
	½ cup port	*Salt and pepper*

VEGETABLES

12 each baby carrots, turnips, cauliflower florets, broccoli florets, baby yellow zucchini, asparagus tips, and snow pea pods

1 tbsp butter	*1 tbsp chopped fresh parsley*	*Salt and pepper*

FILETS

6 filet mignons (2 lb total)	*¾ tsp each salt and pepper*	*1 tbsp each butter and vegetable oil*
2 cloves garlic, minced	*1 tsp fines herbes*	*¼ cup red wine*

• SAUCE: In large saucepan, heat oil over medium heat. Stir in shallots and garlic; cook, stirring often, for 3 minutes or until translucent. Add carrot and celery; cook for 7 to 10 minutes or until softened. Stir in tomato paste and sugar; bring to boil and boil for 1 minute. Stir in port, bay leaf, and rosemary; return to boil and boil for 5 minutes or until liquid is reduced and syrupy. Strain out flavoring agents and return liquid to pot. Stir in beef stock and bring to boil; reduce heat and simmer for 35 minutes or until thickened and reduced to about 1¼ cups. Reduce heat to low and whisk in butter, bit by bit, until butter is fully incorporated and sauce is glossy. Season to taste with salt and pepper. Set aside and keep warm.

• VEGETABLES: In large pot of boiling salted water, cook carrots and turnips for 7 minutes; remove with slotted spoon and place in cold water. Reserve. To same pot of water, add cauliflower and cook for 5 minutes; remove and add to reserved vegetables. Place broccoli, zucchini, and asparagus in boiling water and cook for 4 minutes; add snow peas and cook for 1 minute. Remove and add to reserved vegetables.

• FILETS: Rub meat with garlic, salt, pepper, and fines herbes. In large skillet, melt butter with vegetable oil over medium-high heat; add filet mignons, placing them at least ½ inch apart. Cook, turning once, for 10 to 12 minutes or until meat is well browned but still pink in center. Remove from pan; tent with foil and let stand for about 5 minutes. Add red wine

The sauce recipe I offer here differs from the one I made in the White House kitchen in that it reduces very quickly — not over the course of a day. For this reason, I have added robustly flavored ingredients to reproduce the complexity of a long-simmered sauce.

to hot pan and cook, stirring, to scrape up cooked-on bits for 30 seconds; strain through fine-mesh sieve into reserved sauce. Stir well to combine.

• In large skillet, melt 1 tbsp butter over medium-high heat. Add vegetables and shake to coat in butter; cover and cook, shaking often, for 2 minutes or until vegetables are glossy and heated through. Toss with parsley; season with salt and pepper to taste. To serve, place spoonful of vegetables on each plate. Place filet alongside and cordon sauce around front. Makes 6 servings.

TIPS:

•*It's better to use two skillets to cook the meat than to crowd the steaks into one pan. If the steaks are too close together, they will steam and not brown properly.*

•*Fines herbes is a combination of dried tarragon, chervil, parsley, and chives, which was popularized by southern French chefs. It can be found at gourmet food shops and many supermarkets.*

Jackie was delighted by Casals' words as well as his music.

A classic galantine was composed of a piece of meat filled with forcemeat, a meat-based stuffing containing pork fat and offal. My recipe is a simplified, lighter version made with a vegetable-based stuffing, which should suit modern tastes.

GALANTINE DE FAISAN AU PORTO

STUFFING

1 tsp vegetable oil

4 strips bacon, finely chopped

¹/₃ cup finely chopped shallots

2 cloves garlic, minced

¹/₄ tsp each ground allspice and nutmeg

Salt and pepper

¹/₃ cup port

2 each carrots and celery stalks

GALANTINES

2 cups blanched drained spinach leaves

3 pheasants (or 6 chicken breasts)

1 cup port

6 cups game stock or dark chicken stock (approx)

¹/₄ tsp each salt and pepper

2 tsp unflavored gelatin (approx)

Parsley sprigs

• STUFFING: In skillet, heat oil over medium-high heat. Add bacon and cook, stirring, for 2 minutes. Pour off all but 1 tbsp fat and reduce heat to medium. Add shallots and garlic; cook, stirring often, for 5 minutes. Stir in allspice, nutmeg, and ¹/₄ tsp each salt and pepper. Stir in port; cook, stirring to scrape up any brown bits, for 1 minute. Let cool to room temperature.

• Using mandolin or other hand-held slicer, or sharp knife, cut carrots and celery into long, very thin pieces. In boiling salted water, cook separately for 2 minutes each; cool to room temperature under cold running water. Drain well; pat dry with paper towel and sprinkle with salt and pepper. Reserve.

• GALANTINES: remove skin from pheasants and discard. Cut off wings and legs and reserve. Using boning knife, carefully remove breast from each pheasant in one piece. Starting with rib cage and working down, ease knife between bones and flesh, working from chest to back. After separating meat from rib cage, remove any stray small bones. Halve breasts at natural division.

• Place bones, legs, and wings on well-oiled rimmed baking sheet; roast in 375°F oven for 25 minutes or until browned. Reserve.

• Using side of cleaver or tenderizing mallet, gently flatten each breast to uniform thickness. Rub reserved bacon-shallot mixture evenly over inside of each breast. Flatten a spinach leaf; leaving narrow border around edge of meat, cover the bacon mixture on each breast. Top evenly with carrots and celery. Roll each breast into tight cylinder; roll tightly in cheesecloth, smoothing out any creases. Tie ends with kitchen string.

- Place galantines in large pot over medium-high heat. Add browned bones, wings, and legs. Add port and just enough stock to cover. Bring to boil; reduce heat to low and gently poach for 30 minutes. Remove galantines and cool to room temperature, reserving cooking liquid. Cover galantines with foil and refrigerate for 2 hours or until well chilled.

- Meanwhile, strain reserved cooking liquid through fine-mesh sieve and clarify (see p. 113) to produce consommé. Season well with salt and pepper. Set aside 1¹/₂ cups. Pour remaining consommé into shallow pan and chill until set. (If consommé does not set, re-heat all the consommé and add gelatin; chill until set.)

- Unwrap galantines and slice into ¹/₂-inch medallions; season lightly with salt and pepper. Dip medallions into reserved consommé and place on waxed paper-lined baking sheet; chill for 15 minutes or until jelly is set. Repeat process several times until medallions are thoroughly coated.

- To serve, dip bottom of baking sheet containing jellied aspic in hot water for about 15 seconds; invert onto clean cutting board and chop into small cubes. Arrange cubes on platter; top with medallions. Garnish with parsley. Makes 6 servings.

TIP: *If using chicken breasts, add some chicken bones or necks to the poaching liquid.*

SALADE VERTE

1 head Boston lettuce

1 bunch watercress

2 cooked beets, cut into long, thin strips

12 blanched asparagus tips

DRESSING

¹/₄ tsp each salt and white pepper

Pinch granulated sugar

3 tbsp fresh lemon juice

1 tbsp finely chopped shallots

¹/₃ cup extra virgin olive oil

Asparagus tips and sliced beets add flair to this green salad.

- Wash and remove tough stems from lettuce and watercress. Drain leaves well and place in shallow serving bowl.

- DRESSING: In separate bowl, combine salt, pepper, and sugar; whisk in lemon juice and shallots. Whisking constantly, drizzle oil into lemon mixture and whisk until well combined. Taste and adjust seasoning if necessary.

- In separate small bowls, toss beets and asparagus with 1 tbsp each of the dressing. Drizzle remaining dressing over greens and toss gently. Arrange beets and asparagus tips decoratively on top. Serve immediately. Makes 6 servings.

SORBET AU CHAMPAGNE

Sorbets are fashionable again today as refreshing, light desserts.

2 cups champagne or dry sparkling wine

¹/₂ cup Simple Syrup (recipe follows)

¹/₄ tsp fresh lemon juice

1 egg white

• Stir together champagne, Simple Syrup, and lemon juice. Beat egg white until stiff; gently whisk into champagne mixture until well combined.

• Pour into ice-cream machine and freeze according to manufacturer's instructions. (Alternatively, pour mixture into chilled shallow metal pan; cover and freeze for about 2 hours or until firm. Break up into chunks; transfer to food processor and purée just until smooth.) Spoon into chilled airtight container; freeze for 20 minutes or until almost firm. If making ahead, soften in refrigerator for 10 minutes before serving. Serve in chilled champagne glasses. Makes 6 to 8 servings.

SIMPLE SYRUP

¹/₂ cup granulated sugar

¹/₄ cup water

• In small saucepan, mix sugar with water over medium heat; cook, stirring often, until sugar is completely dissolved. Bring to boil and cook for about 1 minute or until syrup is sparklingly clear. Let cool. (Syrup can be refrigerated in sterilized container for up to 1 month.) Makes ¹/₂ cup.

PÂTISSERIE

• For the Casals dinner, we prepared a selection of freshly baked petits fours, including chocolate truffles, bite-size fresh fruit tarts, madeleines, and tiny cakes encased in rolled fondant and adorned with candied violets.

A relaxed Jackie chats with guests at the private reception held in the Red Room after the concert.

MUSIC, MUSIC, MUSIC

❧

A WHITE HOUSE CONCERT SERIES FOR CHILDREN FEATURING YOUNG performers was just one of Jackie's ideas for supporting the arts. The second Musical Program for Youth concert on February 7, 1962, showcased members of the Metropolitan Opera Studio (below left) in an abridged version of Mozart's *Cosi Fan Tutte*. Afterwards, the colorfully costumed cast joined the audience of embassy children for sandwiches and cake. One singer stood too close to a candle wall sconce and in moments his plumes and turban were ablaze. A thorough dousing from a

nearby milk pitcher quickly put out the flames, but the pungent aroma that permeated the room was distinctive, to say the least. Two weeks later a white-tie audience in the East Room was held spellbound by the rich, velvety voice of mezzo-soprano Grace Bumbry (opposite) in a concert that marked her American debut. Another unforgettable musical moment had occurred three months earlier at a private dinner in honor of President and Mrs. Truman. After a performance by pianist Eugene List, the former president (above) played from memory a favorite Paderewski minuet.

President Kennedy congratulates Grace Bumbry after her stirring performance at a White House dinner for the Vice-President, House Speaker, and Chief Justice on February 20, 1962.

CHAPTER FOUR

THE FIRST LADY AND THE EMPRESS

APRIL 11, 1962

Jacqueline Kennedy's understated elegance on the night of the Iranian
royal visit upstaged even the dazzling, jewel-laden Empress.

WHAT DO YOU WEAR WHEN AN EMPRESS is coming to dinner? We all wondered what Jackie's answer would be as the day for the state dinner in honor of the Shah of Iran and his lovely young wife, Farah Diba, drew closer. Rumors had reached Washington that the Empress would be bringing a stunning wardrobe with her, as well as every major gem from the royal vaults. She obviously hoped to outshine the American President's wife, who was by now world-famous for her chic fashion sense.

Farah Diba arrived that night looking every inch the empress. Gold paillettes woven into the sheer gold fabric of her full-skirted Dior ball gown shimmered as she entered the White House. Crowning her upswept dark hair was an elaborate diamond tiara, studded with priceless emeralds the size of robins' eggs. A necklace and bracelet that matched her tiara and a diagonal ribboned order caught at her shoulder by another explosion of gems completed her fabulous attire.

Jackie played it just right. She wore a sleeveless dress with a white satin bodice and a pale pink heavy silk skirt, very *jeune fille*. She had borrowed some impressive jewelry to wear that evening, but it wouldn't compare to Her Imperial Majesty's, and in any case it didn't feel right. Instead, she decided on a simple pair of diamond drop earrings and a single diamond spray centered in her brioche-styled coiffure, designed by Alexandre of Paris.

I was talking to the President in the family quarters when the buzzer gave the signal that the limousine carrying the Iranian royals would be arriving within three minutes. Two minutes later Jackie came rushing out of her dressing room, her hairdresser still spraying her upswept hairdo, with Provie holding a towel over her dress to keep it from being sprayed, too. She was expecting her husband to lecture her on her habitual tardiness. Instead, the President looked her up and down slowly, smiled, and said in a low voice, "You look so positively beautiful. You look so wonderful." Then he gave a piercing construction worker's kind of whistle, which must have carried two stories below. Jackie laughed with pleasure and down in the elevator they went to greet Their Imperial Majesties.

The Kennedys met the royal couple at the north portico and escorted them upstairs for a half

This occasion marked the first appearance of the brioche (top), an original hairdo by Alexandre of Paris, reinterpreted by Kenneth, Jackie's New York hairdresser. Her Cassini-designed dress (right) was unadorned, save for a simple bow and an arrangement of brilliants around the waist.

hour of private conversation before going down to greet the other guests and have dinner. An excited pair of youngsters in their pajamas, all bathed and brushed, had been promised a peek at the Shah and his Empress before bedtime. The exotic visitors, themselves the parents of a young child, were equally interested in meeting Caroline and John. The Empress had presents for the young Kennedys, which of course made her even more welcome. John just stared, but Caroline curtsied flawlessly, and then turned her attention to the Empress's fantastic jewels. In her mind, her mother probably could not compete at all with the "sparkling gold lady," but to those of us on the White House staff, as well as to the guests and press corps, Jacqueline Kennedy won the contest that night hands down.

During the state dinner, President Kennedy acknowledged the beauty of the two first ladies by beginning his toast with: "His Imperial Majesty and I have a 'burden' that we carry in common; we both paid visits to Paris last year, and from all accounts we might as well both have stayed at home." The Shah's return toast was so long that it delayed dinner, a not uncommon problem for René. After a sumptuous meal, the ninety guests were served coffee and champagne in the Red, Blue, and Green Rooms prior to the evening's entertainment.

The portable stage with its burgundy velvet-covered panels had been set up in the East Room for a performance of selections from Jerome Robbins's acclaimed Ballets: U.S.A., a contemporary company Jackie had seen perform in Europe and again in New York. The seventeen dancers had to contend with somewhat unusual stage conditions. At the dress rehearsal, as one young woman was lifted on high by her partner, she was forced to curve her back like a hairpin to avoid being knocked senseless by one of the giant crystal chandeliers. Mr. Robbins had to adjust his choreography to take into account the low-hanging light fixtures.

Caroline, who attended the rehearsal with her mother, was more concerned with the performers' costumes than their safety. The sweatshirts and black leotards they wore totally confused her. "When are they going to change into their costumes?" she kept asking. Caroline wasn't the only one to notice their tight-fitting attire. Vice President Lyndon B. Johnson commented on the muscular male dancers after the performance. "They make me feel flabby," he complained to Jackie.

At the program's conclusion, the Kennedys and their guests of honor went up on the stage to congratulate Mr. Robbins and the dancers. "You were so wonderful," enthused Jackie, while the President shook hands with each member of the troupe. The Kennedys then escorted the Shah and Empress to the front door of the White House, chatting with them for a few moments before saying good night and returning to their other guests in the hall. Just before midnight, our own "royal" couple retired for the night, another page of history turned and another glittering evening behind them.

The East Room's giant low-hanging chandeliers proved a challenge for Jerome Robbins's Ballets: U.S.A.,
who provided the evening's entertainment. (Opposite) The next day, Jackie gave the Empress a tour of
the White House grounds. Mrs. Kennedy is leading Caroline's pony, Macaroni.

AN EVENING WITH THE NOBEL LAUREATES

APRIL 29, 1962

"I think this is the most extraordinary collection of talent,

of human knowledge, that has ever been gathered together

at the White House, with the possible exception of when

Thomas Jefferson dined alone."

— President Kennedy in his dinner toast

AMONG THE MANY, MANY FIRSTS IN WHITE HOUSE ENTERTAINMENT during the Kennedy years were poetry readings and performances of Shakespeare, opera, ballet, and jazz. As well, the Kennedys were the first to hold youth concerts to encourage young people to study music. The reasons behind some of their receptions, lunches, and dinners were unique as well. For example, they hosted the first reception for all the living recipients of the Congressional Medal of Honor, an incredibly moving occasion.

(Left) Chemist Linus Pauling leads an impromptu waltz in the main hall.
(Above) The President and First Lady are flanked by Pearl Buck and Robert Frost.

The President and First Lady were intellectuals and amateur historians. Unlike most Americans, each year they knew the names of all the winners of the Nobel Prize in the Western Hemisphere and were familiar with their work. One of their very best ideas was to host the first White House dinner in honor of these extraordinary people. It was one of many ways the President found to salute the quality of excellence about which he cared so much.

My social office used our own code name — not a very dignified one, admittedly — for the Nobel Prize evening. We referred to it as the Brains Dinner. René overheard me discussing the Brains Dinner one day and came up to me looking somewhat agitated. "*Non, non, Mademoiselle,*" he strongly protested, "*on ne sert pas des cervelles ce soir-là*" ("We are not serving brains for that dinner"). I assured him that we were *inviting* brains, not serving them.

The staff had preconceived ideas about the guests: we imagined a group of wacky old professors wearing tennis shoes with their evening clothes. How wrong we were. Although the guest list held the names of some of the most distinguished men and women in the sciences, education, government, and the arts, it included a goodly number of well-dressed, fun-loving swingers.

Two widows were asked to represent their husbands at the party. Mary Hemingway graciously gave her permission for an excerpt from an unpublished Ernest Hemingway novel to be read to the guests after dinner. Mrs. George C. Marshall, the widow of General George Marshall, was also invited. Her husband had been awarded the Nobel Peace Prize in 1953 for the Marshall Plan, which provided economic assistance to war-torn Europe. When I

telephoned Mrs. Marshall at her North Carolina home to invite her, she almost burst into tears. "But I never go anywhere anymore," she said. "My health won't permit it."

"You have to come to this," I replied. "The General would want you to. We'll send a plane for you. The Army and our country owe your husband's memory that much."

Also appearing on the list of distinguished names were authors Pearl Buck, John Dos Passos, and Katherine Anne Porter, poet Robert Frost, astronaut John Glenn, future Canadian Prime Minister Lester B. Pearson, and two very controversial scientists. The inclusion of Dr. Linus C. Pauling and Dr. J. Robert Oppenheimer caused some eyebrow-raising on Capitol Hill. The former was a critic of nuclear testing; the latter had helped develop the atomic bomb and eight years previously had come under the scrutiny of Congress and the Atomic Energy Commission. Dr. Oppenheimer's invitation was considered by political pundits as a sign that the present administration might be willing to restore the scientist's security clearance. Dr. Pauling, on the other hand, picketed the White House the afternoon of the dinner with a ban-the-bomb group, much to Jackie's dismay. She gave him a flash of her "mother first, diplomat second" temper. The picketers had kept Caroline awake at naptime, and when Jackie met the tall white-haired scientist that evening, she asked, "Do you think it's right to picket out there where Caroline can see you?"

After the 175 guests arrived on the evening of April 29, 1962, they were announced at the entrance to the East Room. They immediately sought out acquaintances and friends and introduced themselves warmly to strangers. They were a lively,

Soft green jersey was gathered into Grecian lines to make Jackie's asymmetrical evening gown. (Right) the presidential couple greets actor Frederic March.

∽

"Jack and Jackie actually shimmered. *You would have had to be abnormal, perhaps psychotic, to be immune to their dumbfounding appeal. Even Republicans were gaga. They were truly the golden couple...."*

— William Styron, *Vanity Fair*

(Left) Mrs. Kennedy offers her hand in the receiving line. (Top right) My behind-the-scenes duties included directing dinner guests to their places. (Bottom right) The president chats with Pearl Buck and Lester B. Pearson.

friendly group, not at all shy about helping themselves to the trays of drinks offered to them. In no time at all the black-tie gathering had taken on the flavor of a casual cocktail party, with much laughter and lighthearted chatter. One couldn't help but notice some strange party twosomes. What could astronaut Colonel John Glenn and the elderly poet Robert Frost possibly be discussing so earnestly in the corner?

As the time grew near for the President and Mrs. Kennedy to join their guests, the room grew even more animated, only to fall silent in happy anticipation after a fanfare of trumpets and the playing of "Hail to the Chief" announced the couple's arrival. Author William Styron described the Kennedys' entrance in a *Vanity Fair* article: "Jack and Jackie actually *shimmered*. You would have had to be abnormal, perhaps psychotic, to be immune to their dumbfounding appeal. Even Republicans were gaga. They were truly the golden couple, and I am not trying to play down my own sense of wonder when I note that a number of the guests, male and female, appeared so affected by the glamour that their eyes took on a goofy, catatonic glaze."

Jackie and JFK did look marvelous that night. After a recent Palm Beach vacation, they were both deeply tanned. Her sea-foam green Cassini gown fell in soft pleats from one shoulder across the bodice, the off-shoulder style accentuating her lovely neck. He looked fit, relaxed, and handsome, as always.

After the usual protocol procedure — the guests passed through the receiving line in the East Room, then into the main corridor and into the two rooms to be used for dinner — there was some logistical confusion. This was one of the largest dinners attempted inside the State Dining Room and the Blue Room. There were more tables than usual, they were pushed close together, and the wait staff had complained loudly prior to the dinner that they wouldn't be able to wedge into the tiny spaces between place settings to serve people with their usual grace. As the guests tried to find their places, the military social aides and my staff directed traffic into the two rooms. Each guest had been handed a little table card upon arriving with the table number and the name of the room where he or she was to sit. As always, we split up husbands and wives, not only at different tables, but often in different rooms. A woman guest in the Blue Room came up to me in a fury. "Just why am I not seated with my husband?" she demanded. "And why did you give him a good seat in the State Dining Room while I'm stuck off here in Siberia? I'm supposed to be with him!" She was turning various shades of pink, red, and purple like an agitated chameleon.

"Mrs. — ," I said, "you have not been given a seat in Siberia. You have been given an extraordinarily fine seat in this room. The President is the host in the State Dining Room, and Mrs. Kennedy is the host in this room. There she is. You are sitting in full view of her, and you have four very famous people at your table, whom you can go back home and talk about for the rest of your life."

"Oh," she said, all confused, "but I thought husbands were supposed to sit next to wives."

"Not in the great houses of the world," I retorted. To myself I said, "That ought to fix her," but then I decided to push in the thorns a bit deeper. "Of course, if you still want to go into the State Dining Room, I can give you the seat in there of an official who would give anything to be able to change with you, to be at this table with these famous names, and to be this close to Mrs. Kennedy. I'll go switch your seats right now."

She reached out both arms and imprisoned me. "No," she said, docile as a lamb, "this place will do very nicely for me. I'll tell my husband about this table later tonight."

"That's exactly how it's supposed to work," I replied.

In an article for *The New Yorker*, author Diana Trilling recalled her dinner companion: "Dr. Stanley picked up my [place] card. I said, 'You haven't the vaguest idea who I am. You scientists don't read.' He loved my introducing myself that way. He spent the entire dinner trying to persuade me to stop smoking . . . . It was so relaxed in the dining room that I was able to smoke through the entire meal. Nearly everybody was smoking, including most of the women. But Dr. Stanley kept taking my cigarette out of my mouth." The embargo against Cuba had not yet taken effect, so the fragrant aroma of Havanas, the President's favorite, although illegal, cigars, began to punctuate the air as the coffee was served.

(Left) Deep in conversation with Mrs. Ernest Hemingway, a thoughtful JFK seems to mirror an earlier president. (Above) In a rare public show of affection, he drapes his arm around his wife's shoulders as they chat with Pearl Buck. (Below) Robert Frost holds court in the Red Room after dinner. (Opposite) Frederic March.

❧

Earlier in the day Lester B. Pearson had remarked to the President that a Canadian newspaperman had called the dinner "the President's Easter egghead roll on the White House lawn." In his now famous post-dinner remarks, the President referred to the quotation, then added his own description of the brainy individuals seated around him: "I think this is the most extraordinary collection of talent, of human knowledge, that has ever been gathered together at the White House, with the possible exception of when Thomas Jefferson dined alone." William Styron remembered that "the Nobelists roared their appreciation at this elegant bouquet, and I sensed the words passing into immortality."

By this point in the evening, it was clear that our guests were not people who stood on ceremony. So at home were they that they began exchanging autographs and notes on the backs of their menus and place cards like graduates at a commencement dinner. Women searched their evening bags and men rummaged in the pockets of their tuxes for a pen; those that were found were eagerly passed from hand to hand. The Air Force Strolling Strings led the diners into the hall, and although the fast-paced music was meant to entertain the guests as they made their way into the East Room, it proved too much for some of them. We all knew how to waltz in those days, even distinguished Nobel laureates, and several of them, led by the irrepressible Dr. Pauling, began to swing their wives or dinner partners over the polished

marble floor. I sputtered and muttered to no avail, and for a while, it looked as though our terribly high powered intellectual dinner had metamorphosed into a waltz-a-thon. Fortunately, after thirty minutes, we were able to break it up.

During the impromptu dancing, I had taken Frederic March upstairs to the Lincoln bedroom to compose himself before his reading of excerpts from the works of Hemingway, General Marshall,

"[Frederic March] told me later that he had played in palaces and before many distinguished audiences in his life, but never had anything meant so much to him as this night."

— Letitia Baldrige

and Sinclair Lewis. The Lincoln bedroom was always treated with great reverence by citizens and presidents alike during those years. After showing the famous actor to the door, I said, "I'll be back in twenty-five minutes. Here, lie down on the bed — there's a white bedspread. Don't worry about it. Just take off your shoes. There's a blanket, too."

He motioned to the enormous, intricately carved rosewood bed. "You mean, I'm to lie down on *that*, Lincoln's bed?"

"Yes, special orders from Mrs. Kennedy. This is a sacred place — for Abraham Lincoln's ghost and you."

"It is logical that the United States should do whatever it is able to do to assist in the return of normal economic health in the world.... Our policy is directed not against any country or doctrine, but against hunger, poverty, desperation and chaos."

— Frederic March reads from George C. Marshall's
1947 Harvard commencement address

The East Room audience was mesmerized by Frederic March's delivery of the introduction to Sinclair Lewis's Main Street *(right) and passages from Secretary of State George C. Marshall's Harvard address of 1947, in which he outlined the Marshall Plan (left). The performance closed with a chapter from an unpublished novel by Ernest Hemingway, read here in public for the first time.*

Tears came to his eyes. He told me later that he had played in palaces and before many distinguished audiences in his life, but never had anything meant so much to him as this night. Resting in Lincoln's bed, he said, was the crowning part of the evening for him.

Every guest at that incredible dinner took home special memories to treasure for the rest of their lives. For Mrs. Marshall it was listening to Frederic March read a portion of her husband's Marshall Plan speech in the darkened East Room, a single spotlight shining on the handsome actor's face. Mrs. Hemingway doubtless carried home similar memories, in addition to the recollection of the special kindness shown to her by the President: he had walked over to her after the reading of her husband's work and gently raised her from her chair to introduce her to the audience, who reacted with emotional applause. For William Styron, who was one of several guests invited upstairs to the Oval Room after the party and who tried out the President's rocking chair, it was "the leader of the Free World wreathed in smoke, gently rocking: this was the relaxed and contented image I took away with me when, well after midnight, we wobbled our way homeward from one hell of a party."

AN EVENING WITH THE NOBEL LAUREATES

The presentation of the food served to White House guests was very important to the First Lady. The Pommes Chipp *in this menu, for example, were presented in two napkins folded and shaped like an artichoke. My pastry chef, Ferdinand Louvat, decorated the Bombe Caribienne with* sucre soufflé, *or blown sugar, turning this luscious dessert into a work of art.*

— René Verdon

DINNER

Puligny Montrachet Combetter 1er Cru 1959

Château Mouton Rothschild 1955

Piper Heidsieck 1955

La Couronne de l'Élu Victoria

Filet de boeuf Wellington
Pommes Chipp
Fonds d'artichauts Favorite
Endive Meunière

Bombe Caribienne
Petits fours assortis

The White House
Sunday, April 29, 1962

LA COURONNE DE L'ÉLU VICTORIA

• I created this appetizer to commemorate the achievements of the Nobel Prize winners who were our guests. Its English translation would be "Crowns of Victory." Composed of a delicate seafood mousse — like the Mousse de Sole Amiral on page 72 — the crowns are cooked in individual savarin molds and adorned with morsels of lobster.

FILET DE BOEUF WELLINGTON

This English country-house classic was named after Duke Arthur Wellesley Wellington, the victor over Napoleon at Waterloo. It is almost always served with a Madeira sauce.

3 lb center-cut beef tenderloin (Chateaubriand)	¼ tsp each salt and pepper	8 oz puff pastry (recipe, page 65)* or 1 pkg frozen puff pastry
	1 tbsp vegetable oil	1 egg, beaten

DUXELLE

1 tbsp each butter and vegetable oil	4 cups finely chopped mushrooms (about 10 oz)	Pinch nutmeg
1 tbsp minced shallot		4 oz fois gras (goose liver)
1 clove garlic, minced	¼ tsp each salt and pepper	

* Omit sugar if using recipe on page 65

SAUCE

2 tbsp vegetable oil

¼ cup finely chopped shallots

2 cloves garlic, chopped

1 each carrot and celery stalk, chopped

1 tbsp tomato paste

½ tsp granulated sugar

1 cup Madeira

2 tbsp cognac

1 bay leaf

Sprig each thyme, parsley, and rosemary

4 cups homemade beef stock

2 tbsp cold butter, cubed

1 tsp chopped black truffle, fresh or preserved (optional)

• Trim any fat or gristle from beef; season all over with salt and pepper. In large heavy skillet, heat oil over medium-high heat; cook beef, turning often, for about 45 seconds per side or until browned all over. Transfer to tray; wrap well and refrigerate until completely cold.

• DUXELLE: Meanwhile, add butter and oil to skillet. Stir in shallot and garlic; cook over medium heat, stirring, for 2 minutes. Increase heat to medium-high. Stir in mushrooms, salt, and pepper; cook, stirring, for 5 minutes. Reduce heat to medium; cook for 10 minutes or until liquid is evaporated and mushrooms are browned. Add nutmeg. Stir in foie gras. Remove from heat; refrigerate until completely chilled.

• On lightly floured work surface, roll pastry out into rectangle just big enough to encase beef. Leaving 1-inch border around edge of pastry, spread cooled duxelle mixture evenly over top. Place beef in middle of pastry. Snugly encase with puff pastry as if being gift-wrapped, brushing seams with egg to seal.

• Place bundle, seam side down, on rack set over rimmed baking sheet. Using a sharp knife, make four or five vents in top of pastry. Cover with plastic wrap and refrigerate for 1 hour or until completely chilled.

• SAUCE: Meanwhile, in large saucepan, heat oil over medium heat. Stir in shallots and garlic; cook, stirring often, for 3 minutes or until softened. Add carrot and celery; cook, partially covered and stirring often, for 7 minutes or until very soft but not browned. Stir in tomato paste and sugar; cook for 1 minute. Stir in Madeira, cognac, bay leaf, thyme, parsley, and rosemary; cook for 8 to 10 minutes or until reduced and syrupy. Stir in beef stock and bring to boil; boil for about 50 minutes or until thickened and reduced to about 1 cup liquid. Strain through fine-mesh sieve into clean pot. Over low heat, whisk in butter, bit by bit, until sauce is glossy and thickened. Stir in truffles, if using. Keep warm.

• Place pastry-covered roast in 425°F oven for 10 minutes. Reduce heat to 375°F; roast for 25 minutes or until meat thermometer inserted in center registers 140°F. If pastry begins to scorch, tent loosely with foil.

• Remove from oven; tent with foil and let stand for 10 minutes. Carve thick slices from roast, being careful to avoid being burned as steam trapped inside pastry escapes. Serve with sauce on side. Makes 6 servings.

The Nobel Prize dinner was one of the largest state dinners we held and as such required considerable preparation time.

POMMES CHIPP

2 small baking potatoes	4 to 6 cups vegetable oil	Salt

A classic accompaniment to roasted game and beef, pommes de terre chipp *(game chips) should be lightly seasoned and served very fresh.*

• Peel potatoes. Using mandolin or other hand-held slicer, or food processor fitted with fine slicing blade, slice as thinly as possible into rounds; soak in cold water for 10 minutes to remove excess starch. Drain well and pat dry completely.

• In deep fryer or wok, heat oil over medium-high heat to 375°F, or until hot enough to brown a cube of bread in 10 seconds. Working in batches, fry potatoes for 2 to 3 minutes or until very crisp. With slotted spoon or spider basket, remove from oil and set on paper towels to drain. Sprinkle with salt to taste. Makes about 8 cups.

VARIATIONS

• Use seasoned salt, pepper, chili powder, curry powder, or Parmesan cheese as well as salt.
• Substitute beets, sweet potatoes, or parsnips for the potatoes. Leave out soaking step.

TIP: *The success of any fried dish always depends on the freshness of the oil, so change frying oil frequently and be sure to strain it after each use to prolong freshness.*

Table settings in the State Dining Room.

FONDS D'ARTICHAUTS FAVORITE

3 lemons

2 tbsp all-purpose flour

6 large globe artichokes

12 pencil-thin
asparagus tips

1/4 tsp each salt and
pepper

1/2 cup Cream Sauce
(recipe follows)

6 slices black truffle
(optional)

• Cut 1 lemon in half; slice remaining lemons into quarters. Whisk flour into large pot of salted water; stir in quartered lemons. Cover and bring to boil.

• Meanwhile, working with one artichoke at a time, break stem end from base of artichoke; peel off tough outer leaves and trim remaining leaves about 1/2 inch above base. Rub cut surface with lemon. Using knife, trim around base of artichoke until rounded and smooth; rub well with lemon.

• Immerse artichokes in boiling water mixture; keep submerged by weighing down with lid slightly smaller than diameter of pot. Simmer for about 25 minutes or until fork-tender; drain and immerse in cold water. Drain well. Using spoon, scoop out and discard choke. Place artichokes on ovenproof platter.

• In pot of boiling salted water, blanch asparagus for 4 minutes or until tender; drain and refresh under cold water. Drain well. Prop up two tips in each hollowed-out artichoke base. Place in 250°F oven until warm. Spoon Cream Sauce over artichokes; garnish each plate with slice of truffle (if using). Makes 6 servings.

CREAM SAUCE

1 tbsp butter

1 small onion, chopped

1 small bay leaf

1/2 cup each light chicken
stock, white wine, and
whipping cream

Pinch nutmeg

Salt and white
pepper

• In large saucepan, melt butter over low heat. Stir in onion; cover and cook, stirring often, for 20 minutes or until translucent and very soft. Stir in bay leaf, chicken stock, and white wine; bring to boil. Cook for about 5 minutes or until liquid is reduced to about 1/4 cup. Pass through fine-mesh sieve into clean pan.

• Add whipping cream and bring to boil; cook for 2 minutes or until reduced to about 1/2 cup. Stir in nutmeg; season to taste with salt and pepper. Makes 1/2 cup.

TIPS:
• *If truffles are unavailable, use 1 or 2 oz chopped sautéed wild mushrooms.*
• *Homemade fresh or frozen stock is available at grocery stores and better food shops.*

On the evening of the Nobel Prize dinner, I served this dish with a cream sauce so that the meal would not be too saturated with brown colors.

ENDIVE MEUNIÈRE

3 cups chicken or
vegetable stock

1 bay leaf

3 large heads Belgian
endive

2 tsp fresh lemon juice

2 tbsp unsalted butter

1 tbsp chopped fresh
parsley

Salt and pepper

This classic French vegetable dish looks regal arranged on a china serving platter.

• In non-aluminum saucepan, bring stock and bay leaf to boil over high heat. Slice endive heads in half lengthwise; gently immerse in boiling stock. Reduce heat, cover, and simmer for 6 to 7 minutes or until very tender. Drain well and place on warmed serving dish. Drizzle lemon juice evenly over endive.

• In skillet, melt butter over medium-high heat; skim off any foam. Cook for 1 to 2 minutes or until golden brown and nutty in aroma. Drizzle over endive. Sprinkle with parsley; season with salt and pepper to taste. Makes 6 servings.

TIP: *If heads of endive are very large, add 1/2 tsp sugar to the cooking water to offset the natural bitterness that occurs when this vegetable matures.*

Butlers prepare the glasses for before-dinner drinks in the Family Dining Room, which was converted to an impromptu pantry before a state dinner.

BOMBE CARIBIENNE

3 cups Tahitian vanilla ice cream (or any good-quality vanilla ice cream)

3/4 cup well-drained crushed pineapple

1/3 cup coconut milk

1 tbsp white rum

1/2 tsp cinnamon

1/2 tsp pure vanilla extract

1/3 cup whipping cream

1/2 cup grenadine syrup

2 egg yolks

- Place ice cream in refrigerator for 15 minutes or until soft enough to spread easily. Meanwhile, chill 4-cup ice-cream or charlotte mold in freezer. (A 4-cup bowl is a fine substitute.)

- Line base and sides of chilled mold evenly with ice cream, smoothing with back of spoon or palette knife to form symmetrically shaped hollow in center. Freeze for 2 hours or until very firm.

- Meanwhile, stir together pineapple, coconut milk, rum, cinnamon, and vanilla. Reserve. Whip cream until soft peaks form. Reserve.

- In small saucepan, bring grenadine to boil over medium heat; boil until liquid registers 239°F (soft-ball stage) on candy thermometer.

- In large bowl, beat egg yolks; gradually add grenadine, beating constantly. Scrape down sides of bowl; beat at medium speed for 5 minutes. Reduce speed to low; beat for about 5 minutes or until mixture has cooled and thickened. Fold in reserved pineapple mixture. Gently fold in whipped cream.

- Remove mold from freezer; fill center with pineapple-cream mixture, packing gently and leveling off with metal spatula or back of knife. Cover with waxed paper, then with tightly fitting lid or plastic wrap. Freeze for 8 hours or overnight.

- To serve, dip mold into basin of warm water for 30 to 60 seconds. Lift out and wipe dry; run point of knife around edge. Invert chilled serving plate over bombe and turn upside down. Lift off mold and decorate as desired. Cut into wedges. Makes 6 to 8 servings.

Because bombe mixtures are so rich, very little garnish is required. Merely add a ruffle of whipped cream, a few edible flowers, or a drizzle of a tangy coulis in a contrasting color before presenting the dessert.

CHAPTER SIX

A DINNER FOR ANDRÉ MALRAUX

MAY 11, 1962

O F ALL THE SOCIAL EVENTS HELD AT THE WHITE HOUSE, THE ONE THAT mattered the most personally to Jackie was the dinner honoring André Malraux, France's distinguished Minister of State for Cultural Affairs. He had been very kind to her at a time of great personal sorrow in his life. Only days before the Kennedys' 1961 state visit to Paris, his two sons were killed in a car accident, yet Minister Malraux courageously set aside his grief to accompany Jackie to various museums. She was deeply moved by this, and the state dinner in his honor was the Kennedys' way of expressing their gratitude. I heard one of her friends say to her, a few weeks before the dinner, "What's so great about Malraux? He isn't even attractive looking." The First Lady shot two thunderbolts straight into the questioner's eyes. "He happens to be a war hero, a brilliant, sensitive writer, and he happens to have a *great* mind." That took care of that.

One night I was going over the guest list for the upcoming dinner with the First Lady when the President joined us in the Oval Room. He took a copy of the list, sank into an armchair, and perused it, frowning.

"Where are the great Americans on this list?" he asked.

I stumbled about, defending the luminaries who were already on the list.

"No, I mean really great Americans, like Charles Lindbergh."

In spite of the criticism the aviator had received later in life because of his isolationist political views, John F. Kennedy thought of him only in terms of his brave solo flight to Paris in 1927. He had accomplished the impossible and had made his country shine in the eyes of the world. Jackie added that she admired Mrs. Lindbergh and her writing, as well, although she confirmed what I already knew — the Lindberghs were so shy and so frightened of the press that they never accepted invitations or attended public gatherings.

Jacqueline Kennedy and André Malraux share a quiet word during the White House dinner held in his honor.

(Above) Jackie was the center of attention during the official photo session.
She had also appeared in this daring pink silk strapless Cassini original (opposite) at a dinner for the
Shah and his wife held at the Iranian embassy the previous month.

"I don't care," said the President. "We need more Charles Lindberghs coming to dinner in this house."

That was it. I was on the telephone the next morning. It took the White House operators an inordinately long time to reach the Lindbergh residence in the country because their address and telephone number were top secret.

Anne Morrow Lindbergh answered the phone. That surprised me, but she was equally surprised to find Washington on the line. "My dear Miss Baldrige," she exclaimed, "how did you reach us? No one knows our number. Oh, dear!"

"The White House operators can reach anyone who is alive," I replied. She laughed. Then I told her that Mrs. Kennedy was a great fan of her writing, which set off a wonderful round of pleased giggles from Mrs. Lindbergh. When I extended the White House dinner invitation, she gasped, then sighed. Her voice was sad.

"You may have heard that we are quite reclusive. Charles will not accept invitations anywhere. We simply do not go out."

"President and Mrs. Kennedy know that," I answered, "but you have no idea how much it means to them to have you come."

The general walked by his wife at that point, and I heard Mrs. Lindbergh whisper to her husband, "It's the White House." The next thing I knew, he was on the telephone.

"You are calling from the White House, Miss Baldrige? How wonderful!" He chuckled with pleasure. His voice was young, lilting. Hearing it I was almost unable to continue speaking. But I managed to tell him that President Kennedy had said, "Of all the people who would do us honor by coming to dinner, the Lindberghs would be number one."

"Did the President really say that?" asked Mr. Lindbergh skeptically.

"He really did. I am telling you the truth."

There was a hushed conversation between husband and wife, then the general spoke into the telephone again.

"We will come."

The Lindberghs were joined at the dinner by more than 160 other guests, many of them well-known figures in the arts world. In addition to being Minister of State for Cultural Affairs, André Malraux

was an esteemed novelist, art historian, aviator, and former underground fighter. In his honor, the guest list included playwrights Thornton Wilder, Arthur Miller, Tennessee Williams, and Paddy Chayefsky, Pulitzer Prize winners Archibald MacLeish and Robert Lowell, Jr., movie director Elia Kazan, artist Andrew Wyeth, actress Julie Harris, and choreographer George Balanchine. It was such a celebrity roster that I wished I had brought an autograph book and swallowed enough pride to use it.

Even among these illustrious people, the attendance of the Lindberghs caused a sensation. They were young-looking and handsome, in spite of

"I suppose all of us wish to participate in all the experiences of life, but he has left us all behind."
— President Kennedy in his dinner toast to the guest of honor, André Malraux

advanced age. Rejected and hurt by the American public in the past, now, suddenly, they were in their President's home, being lionized. The dinner guests mobbed them, but they smiled patiently through it all. More than one person wept upon seeing Lindbergh up close, because the memory of that curly-haired, slim young man in his leather flying jacket stepping out of the *Spirit of St. Louis* at Le Bourget Airport near Paris was an image they would never forget.

The menu had been carefully chosen by Jackie and René to combine spring fare with French flair. The State Dining Room and the Blue

Room continued the spring theme with arrangements of red and white tulips, baby's breath, blue iris, pink sweet peas, and daisies decorating the tables. The scent of lily of the valley and lavender perfumed the air.

As the guests made their way to the tables, it became apparent that, in contrast to the merry-makers at the Nobel Prize winners' dinner, this was a subdued group of people. In an effort to liven the proceedings, the President quipped in his after-dinner toast, "I am very glad to welcome here some of our most distinguished artists. This is becoming a sort of eating place for artists. But they never ask

(Opposite) Seated at JFK's table that evening were Mrs. Hervé Alphand, wife of the French ambassador, at center, and Charles Lindbergh, at right. (Above) The Kennedys' signature floral arrangements added a finishing touch at the Malraux dinner. (Right) The President addresses the diners.

"There have been some great wives in the White House — like Abigail Adams and Dolly Madison — so great you can't think of their husbands, presidents, without thinking of them. It looks like we're having another one now."

— Robert Frost in *Newsweek*, January 1, 1962

us out." His guests laughed in appreciation, but as Arthur Miller explained to Dorothy McCardle of the *Washington Post*, "All these people are used to earning their living by pushing a pencil or a fiddle; they are not used to talking. They are absolutely overwhelmed by being invited."

After the superb dinner, violinist Isaac Stern played in the East Room, accompanied by Eugene Istomin on the piano and Leonard Rose on the cello.

Jackie loved concerts, even though she knew very little about music. The President, on the other hand, enjoyed about five minutes of a classical performance and then would begin dreaming about being out on his sailboat off Hyannisport. On two evenings he had mistaken a pause between movements as the end of the concert and dashed up on stage to congratulate the musician. Each time, the artist whispered — although the entire room heard it — "But Mr. President, the concert isn't over." I, of course, "caught Kennedy hell" for having allowed such a thing to happen. We worked out a code system for the Malraux dinner concert: One of our military social aides, on loan from the Pentagon, was a music expert. I asked him to stand next to me, and when the concert was over, he cued me, I waggled my finger at the President through a slightly open French door close to him, and he jumped up to congratulate the artists, with Mrs. Kennedy trailing behind. If the press had found out about the finger wagging signal, the entire story of the state dinner and the concert would have centered on that.

The concert ended at about eleven-thirty and the guests left the room to mingle in the foyer, although not without some urging. The

EUGENE ISTOMIN
Pianist

ISAAC STERN
Violinist

LEONARD ROSE
'Cellist

In honor of His Excellency
The Minister of State for Cultural Affairs
of the Republic of France
and Madame André Malraux
Friday, May 11, 1962
THE WHITE HOUSE

(Above) Arthur Miller dominates the doorway of the East Room. (Left) On the evening's musical program was Schubert's Trio in B flat major, Opus 99. (Right) The President, Mrs. Kennedy, and Madame Malraux congratulate Isaac Stern.

Kennedys walked out of the East Room, expecting their guests to follow, but found themselves halfway down the hall with nary a guest in sight. White House aides urged the shy party forward, but no one wanted to make the first move. Finally, a few brave souls ventured out and the rest followed. When Isaac Stern made his way into the corridor, he borrowed a violin from one of the Strolling Strings and joined them in an impromptu concert, much to the delight of all present. One of the guests remarked, "If he would put on a red Hungarian military uniform, he could play many gigs in this town at parties." Stern, often called the Prince of Carnegie Hall, made an enormous impression that evening.

Later, the Kennedys had a long talk alone with the Lindberghs in the Red Room. As Jackie passed me to go into the elevator after saying good-night to this very special couple, she whispered, "You know, these are the moments of history I will really remember the rest of my life."

"You have emoluments attached to your job," I said, laughing, "a tremendous responsibility, but many emoluments."

The President and Mrs. Kennedy request the pleasure of the company of Mr. and Mrs. Haddad at dinner on Wednesday, March 27, 1963 at eight o'clock

Mr. and Mrs. William F. Haddad will please present this card at THE SOUTHWEST GATE, The White House March 27, 1963 at 8 o'clock   NOT TRANSFERABLE

Please send response to The Social Secretary The White House at your earliest convenience

On the occasion of the visit of His Majesty The King of Morocco

White Tie

THE PLEASURE OF YOUR COMPANY

AN INVITATION TO A STATE DINNER AT THE KENNEDY WHITE HOUSE WAS THE hottest ticket in town, but not just anyone could receive the coveted envelope (above). Once the Chief of Protocol had compiled a list of all the "must" guests — from a visiting dignitary's entourage to his country's diplomatic corps — the list came to my office. My staff and I then added a few prominent Americans, including some whose ancestors were from the guest of honor's home country. After this initial list was completed, it was passed to the Kennedys, who invariably penciled in representatives from the literary and arts communities (Jackie), and congressional leaders, political fat cats, and friendly newspaper publishers (JFK). Jackie took a particular interest in the guest list for the Malraux dinner (right), and made sure that it included many of the most accomplished figures on the American cultural scene.

MALRAUX DINNER GUEST LIST

The President and Mrs. Kennedy

Monsieur and Madame André Malraux

The Vice President and Mrs. Johnson

His Excellency the French Ambassador and Madame Alphand

Mr. and Mrs. Frederick B. Adams, Jr.

Mr. and Mrs. Hugh D. Auchincloss

Mr. George Balanchine

Mr. and Mrs. Lucius D. Battle

Mr. and Mrs. Samuel N. Behrman

Mr. and Mrs. Saul Bellow

Mr. and Mrs. Leonard Bernstein

The Honorable and Mrs. Charles E. Bohlen

Mr. and Mrs. Raymond Bonham-Carter

Monsieur Stéphane Boudin

Mr. and Mrs. Clinton B. D. Brown

The Honorable and Mrs. McGeorge Bundy

The Honorable and Mrs. William A. M. Burden

Dr. and Mrs. Leonard Carmichael

Mr. and Mrs. Paddy Chayefsky

Mr. T. Jefferson Coolidge, Jr.

The Honorable and Mrs. Philip Coombs

Mr. and Mrs. Gilles Curien

Mr. and Mrs. Gérard de la Villesbrunne

Comtesse Ghislaine de Renty

The Honorable and Mrs. Claude J. Desautels

Count and Countess Adalbert de Segonzac

Mr. and Mrs. René d'Harnoncourt

The Honorable and Mrs. Paul H. Douglas

The Honorable and Mrs. David E. Finley

Mr. Michael V. Forrestal

Dr. and Mrs. Alfred M. Frankfurter

Mr. and Mrs. Manning Gurian (Julie Harris)

Mr. and Mrs. Gilbert A. Harrison

Mr. and Mrs. Bartlett H. Hayes, Jr.

The Honorable and Mrs. August Heckscher

Mr. and Mrs. George E. Herman

Mr. and Mrs. John Hersey

Mr. and Mrs. Arthur A. Houghton

Mr. Eugene Istomin

The Honorable and Mrs. Henry M. Jackson

Mr. and Mrs. Elia Kazan

Mr. and Mrs. Franz Josef Kline

Mr. and Mrs. Samuel J. Lanahan

Francis Lara de Chaban

Mrs. Peter Lawford

The Honorable and Mrs. Claude Lebel

The Honorable and Mrs. Alexis Leger

Mr. Robert Lehman

Mr. and Mrs. Charles A. Lindbergh

Mr. and Mrs. John L. Loeb

Mr. and Mrs. Stanley Loomis

Mr. and Mrs. Robert Lowell, Jr.

Mr. and Mrs. Archibald MacLeish

Mr. and Mrs. André Meyer

Mr. and Mrs. Arthur Miller

Miss Agnes Mongan

Monsieur and Madame Edouard Morot-Sir

The Rev. John Courtney Murray, S.J.

Mr. and Mrs. Alan L. Otten

Miss Geraldine Page

Mademoiselle Danielle Pons

The Honorable Adam Clayton Powell

The Honorable and Mrs. William Proxmire

Mr. and Mrs. Walter F. Prude (Agnes de Mille)

Mr. and Mrs. David Rockefeller

Mr. and Mrs. James J. Rorimer

Mr. and Mrs. Leonard Rose

The Honorable and Mrs. Walter W. Rostow

Mr. and Mrs. Mark Rothko

Mr. Theodore Rousseau, Jr.

Mademoiselle Jeanne Saleil

Mrs. Pierre E. G. Salinger

Mr. and Mrs. Raymond P. Sanders

Mr. and Mrs. Franklin J. Schaffner

The Honorable and Mrs. Arthur Schlesinger, Jr.

Mr. and Mrs. David Schoenbrun

Mr. and Mrs. Irwin Shaw

The Honorable and Mrs. R. Sargent Shriver, Jr.

Mr. and Mrs. Isaac Stern

Mr. and Mrs. Roger L. Stevens

The Honorable Adlai E. Stevenson

Mr. Lee Strasberg

Miss Susan Strasberg

Mr. and Mrs. Allen Tate

Mr. Mark Tobey

Mr. and Mrs. William Tyler

The Honorable and Mrs. Stewart L. Udall

Mr. and Mrs. John Walker III

Mr. and Mrs. Robert Penn Warren

Mr. Thornton Wilder

Mr. Tennessee Williams

Mr. and Mrs. Edmund Wilson

The Honorable and Mrs. Conrad L. Wirth

Mr. and Mrs. Charles B. Wrightsman

Mr. and Mrs. Andrew Wyeth

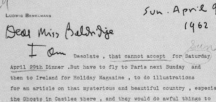

One of the most memorable "regrets" letters I ever received was from Ludwig Bemelmans, creator of the classic Madeline books for children.

A DINNER FOR ANDRÉ MALRAUX

It was an honor for me, as a former citizen of France, to prepare a meal for one of France's most esteemed politicians. Mrs. Kennedy greatly admired Minister Malraux, and we worked together to design a menu that would appeal to him and to the many illustrious guests who would be joining him for dinner. The centerpiece of this dinner was the Bar Farci Polignac, an elegant seafood dish that combines a firm-fleshed fish with the freshness of spinach.

— René Verdon

DINNER

Consommé Madrilène Iranien

Corton
Charlemagne
1959

Homard en Bellevue

Bar Farci Polignac
Pommes Parisienne—
Asperges de Floride

Château
Gruaud-Larose
1955

La Galantine de Faisan au Porto

Dom Pérignon
1952

Le Croquembouche aux Noisettes

The White House
Friday, May 11, 1962

Their pleasure in the occasion is evident in their smiles as JFK and Jackie welcome Monsieur and Madame Malraux.

CONSOMMÉ MADRILÈNE IRANIENNE

7 cups degreased
chicken stock

1 each carrot, leek,
celery stalk, and small red
pepper, all finely chopped

1 tomato, seeded
and chopped

1 tbsp chopped
parsley stems

4 oz extra-lean
ground chicken

3 egg whites, beaten
until frothy

Salt and white pepper

Pinch cayenne

GARNISH

1/2 red pepper, peeled

1 cup chicken stock

Whole flat-leaf
parsley leaves

1/2 cup crème fraîche
or sour cream

2 tbsp caviar

Lemon wedges

This elegant soup is served cold and garnished with crème fraîche and caviar.

• In large saucepan, gently heat stock until it reaches body temperature (98°F on thermometer or test with finger).

• Meanwhile, in large bowl and using rubber spatula, stir together carrot, leek, celery, red pepper, tomato, parsley stems, and chicken until well combined; fold in egg whites. Gently whisk 1 cup of the heated stock into egg mixture.

• Add egg mixture to warm stock; heat slowly, still whisking gently. When mixture begins to look frothy, stop stirring to allow the froth to rise and solidify into raft (clarifying mixture). Return to boil; reduce heat until liquid is barely bubbling. Using end of wooden spoon, carefully make vent hole in raft. Gently simmer for 30 minutes.

• Leaving pot on heat and carefully pushing raft down, ladle clarified consommé into cheesecloth-lined sieve set over bowl. Stir in salt, pepper, and cayenne. Chill until cool but not set.

• GARNISH: Cut red pepper into tiny cubes. In small saucepan, bring chicken stock to boil over medium-high heat; add red pepper and boil for 1 minute or until cooked but still slightly crisp. Drain well; refrigerate until chilled. To serve, divide red pepper and parsley leaves evenly among 6 soup bowls. Ladle equal amounts of chilled consommé into bowls. Float dollop of crème fraîche in center of each bowl, crown with spoonful of caviar. Serve with lemon wedge on side. Makes 6 servings.

"I am glad to welcome here some of our most distinguished artists. This is becoming a sort of eating place for artists. But they never ask us out!"

— President Kennedy, in his toast at the Malraux dinner

HOMARD EN BELLEVUE

❧

The name for this cold lobster dish comes from Madame de Pompadour's country house, where she often entertained her paramour, Louis XV.

ASPIC

4 cups fish stock

3/4 cup dry vermouth or white wine

2 oz boneless white fleshed fish (monk fish, sea bass)

1 egg white

1/2 tsp salt

White pepper

1 pkg powdered unflavored gelatin (1 tbsp)

6 cooked Atlantic lobster tails

SALAD

1 potato, cooked, peeled and finely diced

2 each carrots and white turnips, cooked and finely diced

1 cup cooked green beans, cut into 1/2-inch lengths

3/4 cup mayonnaise

2 tbsp ketchup

2 tsp creamed horseradish

Salt and pepper

GARNISH

Flat leaf parsley leaves

Leaf lettuce

Lemon wedges

• ASPIC: In saucepan, heat stock and vermouth over medium heat to room temperature. In food processor or blender, purée fish until smooth. Beat egg white until stiff but not dry; fold gently into fish. Gently whisk 1 cup of warm stock into fish mixture.

• Stir fish mixture into warm stock; heat slowly, still whisking gently. When mixture begins to look frothy, stop stirring to allow the froth to rise and solidify into raft (clarifying mixture). Return to boil; reduce heat until liquid is just barely bubbling. Using end of wooden spoon, carefully make vent hole in raft. Gently simmer for 20 minutes.

• Leaving pot on heat and carefully pushing raft down, ladle clarified consommé into cheese-cloth-lined sieve set over bowl. Stir in salt and white pepper. Sprinkle gelatin over top; let stand for 2 minutes. Whisk to combine; refrigerate until cold and thickening but not set.

• Meanwhile, remove lobster tails from shells in one piece; slice crosswise into four medallions. Pour any juices out of remaining tail shells; brush shells lightly with thickening aspic. Reserve.

• SALAD: In large bowl, gently stir together potato, carrots, turnips, green beans, mayonnaise, ketchup, and horseradish. Add salt and pepper to taste.

• Divide salad equally among reserved shells. Fan medallions of lobster meat over top of each salad, placing end of parsley leaf between each piece so that leaf lies on top of medallion in front of it. Sprinkle lightly with salt and pepper; brush liberally with aspic, filling in gaps between lobster and shell.

• Place shells on tray; refrigerate for 45 minutes or until aspic is starting to set. Brush with remaining aspic; refrigerate for at least 1 hour or until aspic is well set. To serve, place each tail on bed of lettuce; garnish with lemon. Makes 6 servings.

BAR FARCI POLIGNAC

1 tbsp vegetable oil

2 tbsp finely chopped
shallots

1 small clove garlic,
minced

1/2 tsp salt

1/4 tsp pepper

3 cups stemmed spinach
leaves, lightly packed

1 tsp freshly grated
lemon zest

2 small sea bass
(each 1 1/2 lb)

2 tbsp butter

GARNISH

1 tbsp each butter
and vegetable oil

5 cups sliced
wild mushrooms
(shiitake, oyster)

4 tsp chopped fresh thyme

Lemon wedges

SAUCE

2 tbsp butter

1 leek (white part only),
chopped

1 cup each fish stock,
white wine, and
whipping cream

Salt and white pepper

*This is one of
many French
dishes dedicated
to the Polignac
family. Bar is
a European
name for sea
bass. The
European
variety differs
from the North
American in
that it has no
stripes.*

• In large skillet, heat oil over medium-low heat. Cook shallots and garlic, stirring often, for 5 minutes or until very soft. Stir in salt and pepper. Increase heat to medium-high. Add spinach; cook, stirring often, for 3 minutes or until heated through. Stir in lemon zest. Spread mixture onto rimmed baking tray. Let cool completely.

• Meanwhile, scale and gut fish; remove gills and fins (a good fishmonger will gladly do this for you). Season liberally, inside and out, with salt and pepper. Cover and refrigerate.

• GARNISH: In skillet, heat butter and oil over high heat until very hot. Stir in mushrooms; cook, stirring often, for 2 minutes. Reduce heat to medium-high; stir in thyme. Cook for 5 minutes or until mushrooms are golden brown. Reserve.

• SAUCE: In large saucepan, melt butter over low heat. Stir in leeks; cook, partially covered and stirring often, for 20 minutes or until translucent and very soft. Stir in fish stock and white wine; bring to boil and boil for about 10 minutes or until liquid is reduced to about 1/2 cup. Pass through fine-mesh sieve into clean pan. Reserve.

• Meanwhile, pour off any juices from spinach mixture; divide filling evenly between fish cavities. Dot with half of the butter; press cavities closed and secure with toothpicks or poultry pins. Dot remaining butter over top of fish. Place in buttered roasting pan; bake in 400°F oven for 15 minutes per inch of thickness or until flesh inside cavity is flaky and opaque.

• Stir cream into reduced wine mixture and bring to boil; boil for 7 to 8 minutes or until reduced to about 1 cup. Season to taste with salt and white pepper.

• To serve, re-heat mushrooms and arrange in center of warmed platter. Place fish on top; garnish with lemon wedges. Serve immediately with sauce on side. Makes 6 servings.

POMMES PARISIENNE

❧

• To prepare, simply sautée small round boiled potatoes in butter until golden. Season with salt and pepper and sprinkle with chopped parsley

ASPERGES DE FLORIDE

❧

1/2 cup unsalted butter

2 egg yolks

Salt and white pepper

1 tsp fresh lemon juice

1 1/2 lb young asparagus

1 tbsp chopped fresh parsley

1/4 cup softly whipped cream

• In small saucepan or in microwave, melt butter; using spoon, skim froth from surface and discard. Let butter cool slightly.

The White House kitchen staff took extra care with this very special meal.

• In top of double boiler or metal bowl, whisk shallot mixture, egg yolks, and pinch each of the salt and pepper for 30 seconds or until thoroughly combined, pale yellow, and frothy.

• Over barely simmering water, whisk mixture for 3 minutes or until thickened. Remove from heat; whisk in butter, 1 tbsp at a time, until sauce begins to thicken. Still whisking constantly, pour remaining butter into sauce in slow, steady stream. Stir in lemon juice. Keep warm over pot of warm water. Just before serving, using a rubber spatula, fold in whipped cream. Season to taste with salt and pepper.

• Holding asparagus halfway up stalk, snap off woody ends at natural breaking point; reserve ends for other use. In large pot of boiling salted water, cook asparagus for about 5 minutes or until tender but not limp. Drain well.

• Arrange asparagus on long shallow serving platter; pour sauce across center of stalks, leaving ends showing. Sprinkle parsley over top. Makes 6 servings.

LA GALANTINE DE FAISAN AU PORTO

❧

(see recipe page 76)

LA CROQUEMBOUCHE AUX NOISETTES

❧

• This complex edible pyramid offered my pastry chef, Ferdinand Louvat, the perfect opportunity to showcase his talents. The croquembouche is a cone-shaped edifice of tiny cream puffs, which is built upon a nougat base and then glazed with caramelized sugar. The tower is then decorated with spun sugar and marzipan flowers. The finished croquembouche is a testament to the artistry — and patience — of an accomplished pastry chef. If you choose to serve this classically French confection, it's best to enlist the services of a bakery, as it entails at least a day's work, even for a professional chef.

Not long after Jackie's memorable dinner in his honor, André Malraux agreed to allow the Louvre's masterpiece, the Mona Lisa, *to be exhibited in Washington.*

WHITE HOUSE FIRSTS

RECEIVING VISITING DIGNITARIES ON THE WHITE House lawn instead of at the airport was a Kennedy innovation. The first head of state to be helicoptered to the South Lawn was Ahmed Ben Bella of Algeria, who was greeted with full military honors, on October 15, 1962. Since Ben Bella was a Muslim leader, women did not attend the welcoming ceremony, forcing Jackie to peek from behind the shrubbery (right) with John, Jr.

The first White House presentation of an opera accompanied by an orchestra was planned for the visit of President Radhakrishnan of India on June 3, 1963. A few days before this event, a telephone call from the State Department informed me that the *Magic Flute* costumes of the Washington Opera Society would simply have to go — they were caricatures of Indian dress and would offend Radhakrishnan. Steady rainfall then precipitated another change — we would have to hold the performance indoors instead of on the soggy South

Lawn. But the East Room could not accommodate the stage, the orchestra *and* an audience. The solution was to place the orchestra in the main hall, from where the conductor had to continually turn back and forth from the orchestra to the singers. The production (opposite) went off swimmingly, nonetheless.

A performance of *Brigadoon* for the King of Morocco made me wish that we *had* hidden an orchestra in the hallway. During the

rehearsal, which was watched with great delight by Caroline and her mother (far left), the President stopped by and expressed concern that we were using taped music. I reassured him that all would be fine. Halfway through *Brigadoon* that evening, the fuses blew and the East Room was plunged into total darkness. During the longest minute and half of my life, I heard the President saying, "Your Majesty, it's part of the show, you know." To my intense relief, the power was soon restored and the dancers, who had frozen in their stances, carried right on. At the conclusion of the performance, the President and his guests (bottom left) warmly congratulated the smiling performers.

CHAPTER SEVEN

AT HOME WITH THE KENNEDYS

*Jacqueline Kennedy (opposite) wanted to recapture in the White House the
intimacy of the dinners she had hosted at her Georgetown home (above).*

T HE MATCHBOOKS IN THE KENNEDY WHITE
House were inscribed "The President's
House." Those words captured perfectly
the undeniable fact that the White House was no
longer simply an American institution, but a home,
as well. Nor did the casually graceful style the
Kennedys brought to their new home disappear as
each state dinner drew to a close. The Kennedys'
private dinner dances and intimate black-tie dinners became the talk of Washington and soon the
country.

Held two or three times each year, the dinner
dances were, in the parlance of the day, "swinging"
affairs. Smoky, fun-filled, sophisticated, dance-till-
dawn parties. Sixty or seventy guests would gather
for cocktails in the Red Room and the Blue Room
before sitting down to René's wonderful French cuisine in the State Dining Room. After coffee and
liqueurs, the Kennedys and their guests danced, and
danced, and danced in the candlelit Blue Room to
the lively music of Lester Lanin and his orchestra.

Every ten days or so, Jackie planned a private
dinner party for the President. Rarely were the
guests politicians. "I want my husband to be able to

*The Yellow Oval Room (opposite) was
transformed by Jackie from a presidential study
into an elegant but inviting drawing room.
It was here that such guests as the Mercury
astronauts and their wives were entertained
(Above) American Federal furniture, an Empire
chandelier, and scenic wallpaper were used to
create a handsome private dining room from a
former sitting room (top) on the second floor.*

leave the office, even for a few hours," she told
J.B. West. "I want to surround him with bright
people who can hold his interest and divert his
mind from what's going on over there!" Jackie
worked just as hard on arranging these dinners as
she did the state dinners. Everything had to be just
right, from the food to the table settings. In the
President's Dining Room, she liked to use the
purple-bordered Lincoln china on exquisite white-
on-white embroidered place mats. After she began
to hold these intimate gatherings for up to twen-
ty guests, it became trendy to give small black-tie
dinners instead of large cocktail parties.

Throughout the week, impromptu dinner
parties were held for an even smaller number of
guests, often just a couple or two. Sometimes
invitations weren't extended until the late afternoon. The President frequently didn't know in
the morning whether he would feel like company
that evening. Jackie would check with his secretary, Evelyn Lincoln, in the afternoon to find out
if he wanted guests that evening, and then ask
Evelyn to phone them. Because of the last-
minute timing, the guests were usually old
friends — Toni and Benjamin Bradlee, Bill
Walton or Charles and Martha Bartlett. Charles
Bartlett told journalist Mary Thayer: "It was great
fun to go to the White House to dinner. You'd
arrive about 7:45 and go up to the Oval Room.
JFK would have finished his exercises and his
swim. In the beginning, the swimming pool was
a great novelty to his friends, and they often
would take a swim, too. You'd feel fine as you
sat in the Oval Room with a drink. The President,
who always wore his blue suit, would sit in the
rocking chair by the fire. Then you'd go in to

(Above) Caroline escorted her father to and
from work and often visited the Oval Office with
brother John (below). The President (opposite)
always managed to take "a five minute break"
when the children appeared.

dinner and afterwards to the room at the end of
the hall — which was very cosy. Sometimes
they'd play the phonograph and then, usually
about 10 P.M., JFK would say, 'I've some reading
to do before I go to bed.' And that would be it."

The Kennedys didn't go out very much, pre-
ferring people to come to them. If it seemed at
times as though they were prisoners in their own
home, the family quarters upstairs also afforded
them privacy and protection from "cameras, fans,
and troublemakers," as Mugsy O'Leary said. The
rare overnight guests were pampered with the little touches that make an out-of-town guest feel
welcome. Chocolates, several brands of cigarettes,
and the latest magazines were placed in the guest
rooms (there were seven in all). Entertaining at
home enabled the President to continue his daily
routine. He was usually up at eight. The children's
nanny, Maud Shaw, would bring the children into
his bedroom to visit him while he ate breakfast.
After he had finished, Caroline walked with her
father to his office in the West Wing. At one-thirty
he swam for half an hour, then, if there was no
state function, he went upstairs to eat lunch. While
Caroline and John napped in their rooms, Jackie
would join her husband in his bedroom until
about three when he would return to his office.
On his way "home" in the early evening, the
President would stop for a swim again, sometimes
with the children or friends of the family. He
dressed for dinner and played with Caroline and
John before joining his wife for cocktails. The
adult dinner hour varied from day to day, but was
usually at eight o'clock or later.

Jackie, meanwhile, spent part of the morning
and afternoon with her children, read to them for

"We shall be remembered — we few, we happy few...And

Gentlemen...now abed, shall think themselves accurs'd they were not here."

— A favorite passage of President Kennedy's from Shakespeare's *Henry V*,
read by Basil Rathbone at the White House, April 30, 1963

an hour before dinner, and often sat with them while they ate their dinner at six. When not attending to her family's needs, she worked in the Treaty Room on the second floor. But taking care of her family always came first. Before Caroline and John moved into their new home, she asked the gardeners to make a big snowman on the driveway to greet them. She wanted her children to live as normal a life as possible in the White House and to feel at home there.

René gave Jackie his suggested menus for the day each morning in the kitchen. The children's menus were of particular interest to her. To encourage her son and daughter to try new foods, she asked that the menus include a variety of dishes rather than the usual bland children's fare. This seemed to work, although sometimes with mixed results. René recalls a conversation with Caroline before a luncheon for the Prime Minister of Great Britain, Harold Macmillan. The little girl had been looking at the caviar platters in the kitchen.

"What's that?" she asked.

"That is caviar, my dear," he replied. "It is the tiny eggs of a fish called sturgeon."

"May I have some, please?"

"Well," he cautioned, "most people don't like caviar the first time they taste it."

Caroline thought this over and then said,

"Never mind, then, I'll taste it the second time."

Although the Kennedys had sophisticated palates, they enjoyed comfort foods, as well. Grilled cheese sandwiches had been a favorite of Jackie's since childhood, while the President enjoyed a hot bowl of soup, particularly Boston clam chowder. On one occasion, René remembers him asking for it three days in a row! The Canadian Prime Minister, Lester B. Pearson, was at Hyannisport for a series of meetings. Clam chowder was served on the first day of his visit, and the Prime Minister enjoyed it so much he asked for the recipe. René wasn't surprised, therefore, when the two men asked for it to be served again the following day, but when they also requested it on the third day, he was astonished. The President's father took delight in sending JFK's special favorites to him in the White House, usually via the Kennedy private plane, the *Caroline*. The most eagerly awaited shipments were Joe's Stone Crab from Miami, and exotic flavors of Louis Sherry ice cream, to which Joe Kennedy had unlimited access — he was on Louis Sherry's board of directors.

From sparkling formal dinner dances to casual dinners in their own quarters, the Kennedys' personal style never varied — it was cosmopolitan, modern, and sophisticated, and always peppered with a great sense of humor.

Caroline Kennedy, John F. Kennedy and John Kennedy, Jr., enjoy the Black Watch tattoo on November 13, 1963.

AT HOME WITH THE KENNEDYS

❧

When it came to the menus for meals served to her family and friends, Mrs. Kennedy was no less attentive than for a state dinner. She preferred simple meals prepared with the freshest seasonal ingredients. Caroline and John were not fussy eaters and enjoyed the same cosmopolitan palates as their parents. Like every family, the Kennedys had some favorite dishes — the recipes for a few of them follow.

— René Verdon

The President and I on the day I became a U.S. citizen.

CLAMS JACQUELINE

❧

This is my own invention, a lunchtime appetizer that salutes the First Lady's love of clams.

30 fresh little-neck clams in shell (about 4 lb total)

4 tbsp butter, melted

1/4 cup each chopped fresh watercress and parsley

1/3 cup chopped fresh spinach leaves

2 tsp fresh lemon juice

1 tbsp pernod or Richard apéritif

1/2 cup fresh bread crumbs

1/4 tsp each salt and pepper

• Under cold running water and using clean nylon scrub pad or small brush, scrub clams to remove loose barnacles and dirt. Holding each clam in palm of hand, slide shucking knife between two shells at hinge. Rotate clam until knife reaches hinge on other side. Slide knife along top shell to sever clam from shell. Pull away top shell and discard. Slide knife under clam to separate from bottom shell. Repeat for each clam. Arrange on large rimmed baking sheet.

• In small bowl, stir together 3 tbsp of the butter, the watercress, parsley, spinach, lemon juice, and pernod. Spoon evenly over clams. Sprinkle with bread crumbs; drizzle remaining butter evenly over top. Sprinkle with salt and pepper. Bake in 400°F oven for 7 minutes; broil for 1 minute or until topping is golden brown. Makes 6 servings.

NEW POTATOES AND CAVIAR

∾

1/4 cup olive oil	1/2 tsp each salt and pepper	1 oz caviar
48 tiny new potatoes (about 2 lb total)	1/2 cup crème fraîche or sour cream	Chervil sprigs

• In large roasting pan, heat oil in 400°F oven for 5 minutes.

• Meanwhile, using melon baller, make small cavity in each potato; slice away bottoms so potatoes stand easily. In large bowl, toss together potatoes, salt, and pepper. Place in hot pan and return to oven; bake for 20 minutes, shaking pan occasionally.

• Remove potatoes from oven and let cool to room temperature. Arrange on platter, cavity side up. Just before serving, spoon equal amounts of crème fraîche into potatoes; top each with dab of caviar and sprig of chervil. Makes 48 hors d'oeuvres.

BOSTON CLAM CHOWDER

∾

2 lb little-neck clams in shells (or 1 cup shucked clams)	1 oz salt pork or bacon, cubed	1/2 tsp each salt and pepper
1 tbsp butter	1 onion, finely chopped	1 cup warm milk
	2 potatoes, peeled and diced (about 1 lb)	3/4 cup warm whipping cream

• Under cold running water and using a clean nylon scrub pad or small brush, scrub clams to remove loose barnacles and dirt. Place clams in large deep saucepan; add just enough water to cover. Bring to boil; boil for 5 minutes or until shells open. Strain through fine-mesh sieve set over bowl, reserving broth. Remove clams from shells; chop flesh into 1/2-inch pieces. Reserve.

• In large saucepan, melt butter over medium heat. Add salt pork; cook, stirring often, for 2 to 3 minutes or until just translucent. Add onion; cook, stirring occasionally, for 10 minutes or until translucent but not brown.

• Add potatoes; cook, stirring, for 1 minute. Add reserved broth and bring to a boil; boil for about 8 minutes or until potatoes are fork-tender. Add clams, salt, and pepper; cook for 1 minute or until clams are heated through. Remove from heat; stir in milk and cream. Serve immediately. Makes 6 servings.

TIP: *If re-heating, do not boil.*

Mrs. Kennedy once asked me for a new way to eat caviar, and this recipe proved to be a real conversation piece. Taking their cue from the White House, hostesses all over the United States began serving it at luncheons and dinner parties.

Here is the clam chowder requested by President Kennedy and Prime Minister Pearson three days in a row. I would like to think it played a small part in enhancing U.S./Canada relations.

CREAM OF TOMATO SOUP

1 tbsp vegetable oil

1 onion, chopped

1 celery stalk, chopped

1 tsp granulated sugar

6 cups chopped seeded peeled tomatoes

2 cups chicken stock

¼ cup corn flour

2 cups milk

1 cup whipping cream

½ cup cold butter, cubed

Salt and white pepper

This was a lunchtime favorite of President Kennedy's. I served it to him most often in the summer, when tomatoes are at their very best.

• In large saucepan, heat oil over medium-low heat. Add onion and celery; cook, stirring often, for 10 minutes or until soft and translucent. Add sugar; cook, stirring, for 1 minute or until onion is golden brown. Add tomatoes and chicken stock and bring to boil; reduce heat to medium and simmer gently for 10 minutes.

• Whisk corn flour into milk; stir into tomato mixture until well combined. Simmer for 1 to 2 minutes or until thick enough to lightly coat back of spoon. Stir in cream.

• Transfer mixture to blender; with motor running, add cubes of butter, a few at a time, until fully incorporated and soup is light and frothy. Season with salt and pepper to taste. Pass through fine-mesh sieve into bowl.

• To serve, heat without boiling; ladle into soup cups. Makes 6 lunch servings or 8 appetizer servings.

SPINACH SOUFFLÉ

❧

1/4 cup butter,
plus additional for soufflé
dish

1 tbsp freshly grated
Parmesan cheese

1/4 cup all-purpose flour

1 cup warm milk

1 cup blanched
well-drained spinach
(10 oz fresh)

6 eggs, separated

1/8 tsp each nutmeg and
black pepper

1 tsp salt

• Butter deep 8½-inch soufflé dish to coat evenly; refrigerate for 5 minutes. Remove and butter again lightly; sprinkle with Parmesan cheese, shaking to coat evenly. Discard excess cheese. Return soufflé dish to refrigerator.

• In small saucepan, melt butter over medium heat; sprinkle in flour, stirring constantly. Cook, stirring, for 2 minutes or until flour is golden. Remove from heat and let cool for 2 minutes. Whisk in one third of the milk until completely combined. Add remaining milk and mix well. Return saucepan to heat; cook, stirring constantly, for 3 minutes or until smooth and thickened.

• In food processor or blender, blend spinach with milk mixture until coarsely chopped. With motor running, add egg yolks, nutmeg, and pepper; mix until combined. Return to pan; cook, stirring, for 4 minutes or until thickened.

• In large bowl, beat egg whites with pinch of salt for 3 minutes or until soft peaks form. Using rubber spatula, fold one third into spinach mixture. Gently fold in remaining egg whites and salt until well combined but still streaky.

• Gently scrape into prepared dish; bake in 350°F oven for 30 to 35 minutes or until puffed and golden brown. Serve immediately. Makes 6 servings.

(Opposite) In their pre-White House days, Senator and Mrs. Kennedy entertain their friends Senator John Sherman Cooper and his wife at their Georgetown home. (Right) A plate from the Lincoln service.

❧

Mrs. Kennedy was a well-traveled person who appreciated dishes from all over the world, but, even in private, it was the classics of French cuisine she enjoyed most.

FETTUCCINE RENÉ

Pasta was a Kennedy family favorite. One evening, I devised a new way to prepare it, and Fettuccine René was born.

1 lb fettuccine noodles	*1 cup chicken stock*	*Salt and pepper*
1 tbsp butter	*¹/₂ cup whipping cream*	*2 tbsp chopped chives*
¹/₄ cup finely chopped shallots or onions	*1 cup sour cream*	*¹/₄ cup freshly grated Parmesan cheese*

• In large pot of boiling salted water, cook fettuccine for 8 to 10 minutes or until tender but firm; drain well.

• Meanwhile, in heavy saucepan, melt butter over medium heat. Add shallots; cook, stirring often, for 5 minutes or until softened. Stir in stock and bring to boil; simmer for 5 minutes or until reduced slightly. Whisk in cream; cook for 30 seconds. Remove from heat. Add cooked noodles and sour cream; toss to combine well. Season with salt and pepper to taste.

• Transfer to shallow pasta bowl or deep platter. Scatter chives over top; sprinkle with cheese. Makes 6 servings.

QUICHE PIPERADE BISCAYNE

The President preferred a light lunch, often soup or tiny quiches. This was one of his favorites.

2 tbsp olive oil	*1 clove garlic, minced*	*4 eggs*
1 small onion, chopped	*1 tbsp chopped pimientos or roasted red pepper*	*1¹/₂ cups whipping cream*
1 small green pepper, chopped		*1 tbsp chopped fresh parsley*
2 cups skinned, seeded, and diced tomatoes	*³/₄ tsp each salt and pepper*	*one 10-inch partially baked pie shell (or six 4-inch shells)*
	¹/₂ cup finely chopped smoked ham (about 2 oz)	

• In large deep skillet, heat oil over medium heat. Add onion; cook for 3 minutes. Increase heat to medium-high. Add green pepper; cook, stirring often, for 2 minutes. Add tomatoes, garlic, pimientos, salt, and pepper; cook, stirring occasionally, for 10 minutes. Stir in ham. Remove from heat and cool completely.

• Meanwhile, whisk together eggs and cream; stir in cooled tomato mixture. Pour into partially baked pie shell; sprinkle with parsley. Bake in 425°F oven for 10 minutes. Reduce heat to 350°F; bake for 20 minutes or until set but still jiggly. Makes 6 servings.

PURÉE FAVORITE

1 lb green beans

1 bunch broccoli

1 tbsp butter

1/2 cup whipping cream

Pinch nutmeg

1/2 tsp each salt and pepper

1 tsp lemon juice

• Clean beans and cut in half. Remove florets from broccoli; peel and chop stems coarsely. In pot of boiling salted water, cook vegetables for 10 to 12 minutes or until tender. Drain well.

• In food processor or blender, purée vegetables until very smooth. Using rubber spatula, pass through coarse sieve; return to food processor.

• In small saucepan, heat butter, whipping cream, nutmeg, salt, and pepper until steaming. Pour into vegetables; mix until smooth. Stir in lemon juice. Makes 6 servings.

It is sometimes difficult to make vegetables interesting for children, but Caroline and John especially enjoyed this dish.

PARFAIT AUX FRAMBOISES NOYAU

1 pkg frozen raspberries (10 oz)

2 tbsp unflavored gelatin powder

1/2 cup cold water

1 1/2 cups champagne or sparkling wine

1 1/4 cups granulated sugar

1/2 cup Frangelico or other nut-flavored liqueur

1 cup whipping cream

• Thaw raspberries and press through fine-mesh sieve into saucepan; heat until steaming.

• Meanwhile, sprinkle gelatin over cold water; stir and let stand for 5 minutes. Mix into raspberry purée, stirring until completely dissolved.

• Add champagne, sugar, and liqueur. Refrigerate, stirring often, for about 1 hour or until thick enough to almost hold its shape.

• Whip cream until stiff peaks form. Using rubber spatula, gently and slowly fold into raspberry mixture until well combined. Spoon into serving bowl or 8 parfait cups or dessert bowls. Cover and refrigerate for at least 2 hours or for up to 2 days. Makes 6 to 8 servings.

This rich dessert of raspberries and cream looks innocent enough, but it packs quite a punch.

CHOCOLATE SOUFFLÉ

6 oz bittersweet chocolate

¹/₃ cup butter, plus additional for soufflé dish

6 egg yolks

8 egg whites

¹/₄ tsp cream of tartar

3 tbsp granulated sugar, plus additional for soufflé dish

Confectioner's sugar

This recipe recalls Mrs. Kennedy's — and the children's — love of chocolate.

• Butter inside of 8¹/₂-inch soufflé dish to coat evenly; refrigerate for 5 minutes. Remove and sprinkle with granulated sugar, shaking to coat evenly; discard excess sugar. Refrigerate soufflé dish.

• In bowl over saucepan of hot (not boiling) water, melt chocolate with butter, stirring occasionally. Add egg yolks, whisking constantly until well combined.

• In bowl and using electric mixer, beat egg whites with cream of tartar until soft peaks form. Gradually beat in granulated sugar, 1 tbsp at a time, until stiff peaks form.

• Fold one quarter into chocolate mixture until almost blended; gently fold in remaining egg whites until well combined but still slightly streaky.

• Gently scrape into prepared dish. Place in 425°F oven for 5 minutes. Reduce heat to 400°F; bake for 25 minutes or until puffed and slightly firm to the touch. Dust with confectioner's sugar. Serve immediately. Makes 6 servings.

A celebration for JFK's forty-sixth birthday, held aboard the presidential yacht Sequoia, *included actor David Niven, seen on Jackie's right, and Bill Walton, a pregnant Ethel Kennedy, and Charles Bartlett on her left.*

FLOATING ISLANDS

✣

| 5 eggs, separated | 3 cups milk | 1 tbsp confectioner's sugar |
| 1 cup granulated sugar | 1 1/2 tsp pure vanilla extract | |

• In large bowl, beat egg whites at medium-high speed until foamy. Gradually beat in 3/4 cup of the sugar until stiff peaks form.

• In deep skillet or large saucepan, bring milk to boil. Reduce heat to low; stir in remaining sugar and vanilla.

• Working in batches and using serving spoon, spoon large mounds of egg white into hot milk. Cook for 2 minutes. With slotted spoon, gently turn each mound over and cook for 2 minutes more or until firm to the touch. With slotted spoon, remove cooked meringues to parchment paper-lined baking sheet, reserving milk and keeping hot.

• In large bowl, beat egg yolks at medium-high speed until pale yellow. Gradually beat in reserved milk in slow, steady stream. Return egg mixture to pan; cook over medium-low heat, stirring constantly, for about 5 minutes or until thick enough to coat back of spoon. Strain through fine-mesh sieve into bowl.

• Sprinkle confectioner's sugar over meringues; place under broiler for 45 seconds or until golden brown. To serve, ladle sauce into shallow bowls; place meringues on top. Makes 6 servings.

This dessert was often requested by Mrs. Kennedy when she was dining with family or close friends.

JACKIE'S FRUIT SAUCE

✣

| 1 cup low-fat cottage cheese | 3 tbsp honey | 1 tsp finely grated orange zest |
| 1 cup plain yogurt | 1 tbsp strained fresh lemon juice | Pinch cinnamon |

• In blender, mix cottage cheese, yogurt, honey, lemon juice, orange zest, and cinnamon at high speed until consistency of milk shake. (Sauce can be refrigerated for up to 4 days.) Makes 2 cups.

TIP: *For a change of taste, substitute grenadine for the honey.*

Mrs. Kennedy reserved this sauce for family meals. It was served over berries, peaches, melon, and other fresh fruit.

EPILOGUE

❧

IN THE SUMMER OF 1963 I was physically exhausted and wanted, as well as needed, a change of pace. I had worked twelve and sometimes eighteen-hour days, seven days a week, winter and summer, since November 1960. I'd had no private life, taken no vacations, found no time to think or dream. When the Kennedys were away, I still had work to do — including touring heads of state through the empty house. No foreign leader (and particularly no leader's spouse) could admit they

A pregnant Jackie and I share a smile at the farewell party she gave for me in the White House China Room.

❧

had never seen the White House "under the Kennedys."

As much as I reveled in the euphoria of being part of an exciting time in history, the constant pressure was finally getting to me. After much soul-searching, I decided that after twelve years in government — broken only by my brief stint at Tiffany's — it was time to go off in new directions. Jackie, of course, gave me her blessing. And fortunately she had no trouble finding a replacement.

Nancy Tuckerman, her old friend from New York and Miss Porter's, agreed to take over the job. Jackie was pregnant again with a third child (who, sadly, would live only a few hours) and away for the summer, but, with the help of the wonderful White House staff, a team in every sense of the word, Nancy performed splendidly.

When it came time for me to say good-bye to the people I'd worked with so closely for almost three years, my emotions got the better of me. I wept saying good-bye to René and Ferdinand in the kitchen; to J.B. and his staff; to Anne Lincoln; to Pam Turnure, who handled the press with such agility; to Jackie's personal maid, Provie; and the President's valet, George. And I cried during a good part of the farewell party Jackie and J.B. gave for me in the China Room, where I had spent so much time explaining to so many people the various dinner services the first ladies had ordered to mark their White House tenures. Musicians from the Marine

The Kennedy family on the White House balcony during a
performance of the Black Watch Highland Regiment. Only ten days later I would have the sad responsibility
of arranging for the regiment to return to Washington to play during the President's funeral.

Band accompanied a spirited and very off-key rendition of "Arrivaderci, Tish," with lyrics written by Jackie and sung to the tune of "Arrivaderci, Roma." Greatest song I ever heard. I must have used up an entire box of tissues that day.

Later, when the President said good-bye to me in his office, he told me I was the most emotional woman he'd ever known, but that he considered this a plus, not a minus. He had always counted on me to be cheerful, regardless of what was happening, and he was grateful that Miss Push-and-Pull had kept him in proper protocol shape. "Some day I'd like to congratulate your brothers, Tish," he added. "They've done a good job in raising you."

Those were the last words he spoke to me. My next visit to the White House was a deeply

Even in mourning, Jacqueline Kennedy displayed the grace and poise that had so distinguished her during her husband's days in office. Here she receives the condolences of foreign heads of state in the Red Room.

solemn one, following the tragic events of November 22, 1963, when I came back to help with the ceremonial aspects of the President's funeral.

Even in mourning, Jackie's poise did not desert her. She carried through those awful days with as much dignity as any woman in public life

has ever shown in a time of tragedy. In the eyes of the world, my country looked diminished by the President's assassination. But in the way the funeral was handled, in the way Jackie found the strength to receive each of the world leaders who attended, America raised itself back up.

IN MANY WAYS, THIS BOOK has been a tribute to Jacqueline Kennedy, not just to her sense of style but to the human qualities that made her a memorable First Lady, a loyal wife, a wonderful mother, and a devoted friend. But since this is a book primarily about entertaining, my great wish is that our readers will receive from her example a dose of inspiration and start entertaining at home. We have been doing this less and less as we near the end of the millennium, which is sad, because to entertain is to give of oneself. It's a kindness.

In her private life, before and after the White House, Jackie understood this well. A host helps cheer up those who sit around her table. A host disseminates information and happy gossip, finds solutions to problems, gives everyone many opportunities to laugh or at least smile, and creates a setting where new relationships can evolve into lasting friendships.

We may not be born hosts, like the Kennedys were, but we can keep remembering what a *giving* pursuit the art of entertaining is, and how much better it is to be a giver some of the time than a taker all of the time. And, in retrospect, I must say that no one had a better time at the Kennedys' parties than the hosts themselves. With their appreciation of history unfolding right before their eyes, and with their sense of style, they made an indelible impression on their country and the world.

APPENDIX

❦

Notable Kennedy White House Official Social Events

APRIL 5, 1961: A visit from Prime Minister Harold Macmillan

MAY 3, 1961: State Dinner for President Bourguiba of Tunisia

MAY 24, 1961: Luncheon with Prince Rainier and Princess Grace of Monaco

JULY 11, 1961: State Dinner for President Mohammed Ayub Khan of Pakistan

AUGUST 22, 1961: First Musical Program for Youth: student orchestra from Brevard Music Center, North Carolina

OCTOBER 4, 1961: State Dinner for President Abboud of the Sudan, with entertainment by members of the American Festival Shakespeare Theater

NOVEMBER 1, 1961: Dinner for Former President Truman and Mrs. Truman

NOVEMBER 7, 1961: Dinner for Prime Minister Jawaharlal Nehru of India

NOVEMBER 13, 1961: State Dinner for Governor Muñoz Marin of Puerto Rico, with a performance by Pablo Casals

FEBRUARY 6, 1962: Second Musical Program for Youth: the Metropolitan Opera Studio

FEBRUARY 20, 1962: Dinner for the Vice President, the Speaker and the Chief Justice, with a performance by Grace Bumbry

APRIL 11, 1962: State Dinner for the Shah and Empress of Iran, with a performance by Jerome Robbins' Ballets: U.S.A.

APRIL 16, 1962: Third Musical Program for Youth: the Greater Boston Youth Symphony and the Breckenridge Boys' Choir

APRIL 29, 1962: Dinner for the Nobel Laureates

MAY 11, 1962: Dinner for André Malraux

MAY 22, 1962: State Dinner for the President of the Republic of the Ivory Coast, with a performance of *Billy the Kid* by the American Ballet Theater

AUGUST 6, 1962: Fourth Musical Program for Youth: the Interlochen National Music Camp's orchestra and ballet group

OCTOBER 15, 1962: State Luncheon for Premier Ben Bella of Algeria

NOVEMBER 14, 1962: A visit from Chancellor Konrad Adenauer of the Federal Republic of Germany

NOVEMBER 19, 1962: Fifth Musical Program for Youth: pianist Tong Il Han and the Paul Winter Jazz Sextet

FEBRUARY 12, 1963: Reception on the Centennial of the Emancipation Proclamation

MARCH 27, 1963: State Dinner for King Hassan II of Morocco, with a performance of excerpts from *Brigadoon* by the New York City Center Light Opera Company

APRIL 22, 1963: Sixth Musical Program for Youth: the Berea College Country Dancers and the Central Kentucky Youth Symphony Orchestra

APRIL 30, 1963: State Dinner for the Grand Duchess and Prince of Luxembourg, with a performance by Basil Rathbone and the Consort Players

MAY 2, 1963: Military Reception for all living Congressional Medal of Honor winners

JUNE 3, 1963: State Dinner for President Radhakrishnan of India, with excerpts from *The Magic Flute* by the Opera Society of Washington

SEPTEMBER 5, 1963: State Dinner for the King and Queen of Afghanistan, with a military parade and a spectacular fireworks display

OCTOBER 1, 1963: State Dinner for Haile Selassie, Emperor of Ethiopia, with a dance program by the Robert Joffrey Ballet

OCTOBER 15, 1963: State Dinner for President Seán Lemass of Eire

NOVEMBER 13, 1963: Performance by the Black Watch Tattoo

ACKNOWLEDGMENTS

MADISON PRESS BOOKS AND LETITIA BALDRIGE would like to extend special thanks to Nancy Tuckerman for her invaluable help during the conception of this book and for suggesting the title. We are also grateful for the assistance of Pam Timmins, Oleg Cassini, Rex Scouten, Carl Brandt, Eugene Allan, Edwin Durbin, James Rees and King Laughlin of the Mount Vernon Estate, Anne Garside of the Peabody Institute, and Suzanne Goldstein of Photo Researchers, Inc.

The John F. Kennedy Library is a model for archives everywhere, and we are greatly indebted to its excellent staff including head archivist Will Johnson, June Payne, Maura Porter, and Donna Cotterell, James Hill and Jim Cedroni. Particular thanks are owed to Allan Goodrich for his encyclopedic knowledge of the Library's picture collection and for his courteous and prompt assistance with our many requests.

RENÉ VERDON would like to thank Yvette Verdon, Louis Liberty and Annette Bonnell as well as Dana McCauley and her test kitchen assistants Susan Van Hezewijk, Mara Subotincic and Beatrice Damore.

PHOTOGRAPH AND ILLUSTRATION CREDITS

SELECT BIBLIOGRAPHY

BOOKS AND ARTICLES

Abbott, James A. and Elaine M. Rice. *Designing Camelot: The Kennedy White House Restoration.* New York: Van Nostrand Reinhold, 1998.

Anthony, Carl Sferrazza. *As We Remember Her: Jacqueline Kennedy Onassis in the Words of her Friends and Family.* New York: Harper Collins, 1997.

Baldrige, Letitia. *Of Diamonds and Diplomats.* Boston: Houghton Mifflin Company, 1968.

Cassini, Oleg. *A Thousand Days of Magic: Dressing Jackie Kennedy for the White House.* New York: Rizzoli, 1995.

Kunhardt Jr., Philip B., ed. *LIFE in Camelot: The Kennedy Years.* Boston: Little, Brown and Company, 1988.

Lieberson, Goddard, ed. *John Fitzgerald Kennedy ... As We Remember Him.* New York: Atheneum, 1965.

Lincoln, Anne H. *The Kennedy White House Parties.* New York: The Viking Press, 1967.

Lowe, Jacques. *Jacqueline Kennedy Onassis: A Tribute.* New York: Jacques Lowe Visual Arts Projects, 1995.

Styron, William. "Havanas in Camelot." *Vanity Fair* (July 1996): 32-41.

Suarez, J.C., and J. Spencer Beck. *Uncommon Grace.* Charlottesville, Virginia: Thomasson-Grant, 1994.

Thayer, Mary Van Rensaeler. *Jacqueline Kennedy: The White House Years.* Boston: Little, Brown, 1971.

Trilling, Diana. "A Visit to Camelot." *The New Yorker* (June 2, 1997): 54-65.

Verdon, René. *The White House Chef Cookbook.* New York: Doubleday & Company, Inc., 1968.

West, J.B. *Upstairs at the White House.* New York: Coward, McCann, Geoghegan, 1973.

ORAL HISTORIES

Oral Histories from the John F. Kennedy Library consulted include: Janet Lee Auchincloss, Letitia Baldrige, Grace de Monaco, Maud Shaw, Nancy Tuckerman, Pamela Turnure.

GENERAL INDEX

RECIPE INDEX

DESIGN, TYPOGRAPHY AND
ART DIRECTION
Gordon Sibley Design Inc.

EDITORIAL DIRECTOR
Hugh Brewster

PROJECT EDITOR
Mireille Majoor

EDITORIAL ASSISTANCE
Rick Archbold

TEXT WRITING/EDITING
Laurie Coulter

RECIPE DEVELOPMENT/TESTING
Dana McCauley

PHOTO COORDINATOR
Susan Aihoshi

COVER PHOTOGRAPHY
Clive Champion

PRODUCTION DIRECTOR
Susan Barrable

PRODUCTION COORDINATOR
Donna Chong

COLOR SEPARATION
Colour Technologies

PRINTING AND BINDING
Butler & Tanner Limited

IN THE KENNEDY STYLE

WAS PRODUCED BY
MADISON PRESS BOOKS,
WHICH IS UNDER THE DIRECTION OF
ALBERT E. CUMMINGS